WALT WHITMAN SPEAKS

WALT WHITMAN SPEAKS

HIS FINAL THOUGHTS ON LIFE,
WRITING, SPIRITUALITY,
AND THE PROMISE OF AMERICA
as told to HORACE TRAUBEL

EDITED AND WITH AN INTRODUCTION BY
BRENDA WINEAPPLE

LIBRARY OF AMERICA
Special Publication

WALT WHITMAN SPEAKS

Introduction and volume compilation copyright © 2019 by
Literary Classics of the United States, Inc., New York, N.Y.
All rights reserved.

Published in the United States by Library of America.
www.loa.org

Distributed to the trade in the United States
by Penguin Random House Inc. and in Canada
by Penguin Random House Canada Ltd.

Library of Congress Control Number: 2018962374
ISBN 978–1–59853–614–0

1 3 5 7 9 10 8 6 4 2

Printed in the United States of America

Contents

Introduction

BY BRENDA WINEAPPLE

IN 1855 no one had yet heard anything like the raw, declamatory, and jubilant voice of the self-proclaimed "American, one of the roughs, a kosmos"—that is, Walt Whitman, who famously announced, "I celebrate myself, / And what I assume you shall assume, / For every atom belonging to me as good belongs to you." In his dazzling poetic debut, *Leaves of Grass*, published near the Fourth of July, Whitman was unequivocally declaring his own independence from poetic conventions and niceties. He didn't even include his name on the title page, although on the frontispiece there was a portrait of a bearded man, without cravat, his shirt open, with one hand on his hip, the other in his pocket, and his hat rakishly tipped back. Here was a poet of the people for the people, without pretension or pomp, who wrote in a verse form that captured everyday speech, both its fluency and its clank. "The best writing," Whitman would say, "has no lace on its sleeves."

And, now, in this volume, Whitman again speaks to us, this time from his home at 328 Mickle Street in Camden, New Jersey. "I seem to be developing into a garrulous old man—a talker—a teller of stories," as he told his friend, Horace Traubel, the blue-eyed twenty-nine-year-old who was transcribing in shorthand most of what Whitman said to him during the last years of Whitman's life. By the time Whitman died in 1892, Traubel had accumulated about five thousand pages of these conversations, a monumental chronicle of Whitman's reflections, ruminations, analyses, and affirmations.

In many ways, Whitman and Traubel had been collaborating on a project begun in 1888. Although Whitman didn't know exactly what Traubel was jotting down, he understood that Traubel would write of their relationship one day, telling the trusted younger man, "I want you to speak for me when I am dead." As Whitman further explained, "you will be called on many a time in the future to bear witness—to quote these days, our work together, the talks, anxieties—the victories, defeats. Whatever we do, we must let our history tell the truth: whatever becomes of us, tell the truth." For he didn't want to be mummified. "Do not prettify me: include all the hells and damns," Whitman instructed. And when Traubel read back to Whitman some of what he'd transcribed, as he sometimes did, Whitman replied with satisfaction, "You do the thing just as I should wish it to be done." He had found his very own Boswell.

Whitman had first encountered Horace Traubel about fifteen years earlier, shortly after the poet had arrived in Camden in 1873. Traubel was carrying a large stack of library books, and Whitman had joked about a boy reading too much. They quickly formed a friendship and together they sat on the front stoop to discuss what they'd been reading, or they'd watch baseball games together on the Camden common. Initially, a number of people complained to Traubel's mother that her son shouldn't associate with such an old lecher, but Traubel, who greatly admired the poet and his work, volunteered to run errands for an increasingly infirm Whitman.

Whitman had moved into his brother's home in Camden after suffering a stroke, and though he regained some strength and mobility, he continued staying with his brother's family, where his mother was also then living. After her death, when the rest of the Whitmans left Camden, the poet purchased a small, two-story row house on Mickle Street. By 1888, Traubel was stopping by every day, usually on his way home from nearby Philadelphia, where he worked as a bank clerk. As Whitman's unofficial amanuensis, he answered Whitman's letters, scoured Philadelphia for the kind of pens that Whitman liked, and was soon marshaling Whitman's friends together to help pay for his caregivers and nurses. Traubel arranged benefit lectures to defray their expense, and he organized the birthday dinners and iced champagne that delighted Whitman. Efficient and methodical, Traubel also acted as liaison to several editors when Whitman was preparing his volume, *November Boughs*. For the invaluable Traubel was proficient in matters of manuscript preparation, from printers and binders to publicity and promotion. Whitman entirely trusted him, and with Traubel's able assistance, Whitman published such late volumes as a pocket edition of *Leaves of Grass*, a *Complete Poems and Prose*, the volume *Good-bye My Fancy*, and the "deathbed" edition of *Leaves of Grass*.

Traubel thus brought Whitman light, hope, encouragement, and love. "I wonder whether you understand at all the functions you have come to fulfil here! that you're the only thing between me and death?" Whitman exclaimed in 1889. "That but for your readiness to abet me I'd be stranded beyond rescue?" As the biographer of Whitman, which is essentially what Traubel had become, he also sifted through the heap of manuscripts, letters, books, envelopes, magazines, and slips of paper strewn in apparently willy-nilly fashion all over Whitman's second-floor bedroom. "I live here in a ruin of debris—a ruin of ruins," Whitman sheepishly admitted. If he proposed to burn or tear up a letter, Traubel intervened, often successfully, and whenever the young man asked for some document, Whitman handed it over without protest.

Their routine continued with rare exceptions, and by 1891, Traubel felt so close to the poet that he was married in Whitman's home. Utterly comfortable with one another, Traubel and Whitman could sit together in silence for long periods, but then Traubel might make a remark to encourage Whitman, trying nonetheless "to not trespass and not to ply him too closely with questions necessary or unnecessary," as Traubel later said. But he pushed back against some of Whitman's biases, both men enjoying the give-and-take. For Traubel was a committed socialist, which Whitman decidedly was not. "How much have you looked into the subject of the economic origin of things we call vices, evils, sins?" Traubel gently needled his friend. Smiling, Whitman replied with good humor, "You know how I shy at problems, duties, consciences: you seem to like to trip me with your pertinent impertinences."

In turn, Whitman would tease Traubel, promising him revelations that he never delivered, such as the secret Whitman described as "the one big factor, entanglement (I may almost say tragedy) of my life about which I have not so far talked freely with you." Prodded, Whitman demurred. "Some day the right day will come—then we'll have a big pow-wow about it," he temporized. The right day never came. "There is something furtive in my nature," Whitman once told a friend, "like an old hen." If Whitman did in fact reveal a secret, Traubel didn't record it, although he seems to have recorded everything faithfully and to have fulfilled his promise not to sanitize or to censor.

Whatever Whitman or Traubel may have concealed, Traubel's great achievement did lie in these transcriptions; the first volume, *With Walt Whitman in Camden*, was published in 1906 as a kind of daily diary of Whitman's talk. As the younger man explained, "I have let Whitman alone. I have let him remain the chief figure in his own story. This book is more his book than my book. It talks his words. It reflects his manner. It is the utterance of his faith. That is why I have not fooled with its text. Why I have chosen to leave it in its unpremeditated arrangement of light and shade," he continued. "It was not my purpose to produce a work to dazzle the scholar but to tell a simple story." The result is a Whitman whole, presented informally and without polish, that reveals the breadth of Whitman's interests—from science and literature to petty gossip: "a human phonograph," one reviewer called it. Whitman emerged as spirited and vain, judgmental and broad-minded, stoic and easygoing, and enduringly warmhearted. In fact, he was not unlike the courageous and brash poet who promised back in 1855 "a perpetual journey," perpetually unfolding in a verse where "past and present and future are not disjoined":

> . . . I do not talk of the beginning or the end.
> There never was any more inception than there
>   is now,
> Nor any more youth or age than there is now,
> And will never be any more perfection than there
>   is now,
> Nor any more heaven or hell than there is now.

———

Ralph Waldo Emerson had lobbied for an American poet who cared less about decorous meters than a meter-making argument, a self-reliant poet who articulated the new age and helped bring it into being. But not even Emerson had dared imagine the "barbaric yawp" that Whitman was to sound "over the roofs of the world."

Whitman hurled each single line forward—often a very long line that vibrated with internal rhythm. To sing of what he saw and where he went, he invented words or borrowed them from other languages as he sailed along. And he delighted in grammar, unleashing prepositions and conjunctions and participles that suggested connection and movement. "I was simmering, simmering, simmering," Whitman reportedly said. "Emerson brought me to a boil."

Although Whitman would later minimize his debt to Emerson, he did share with him the belief that, as Whitman said, "a poem must each time be a new discovery—not seem old, stale, *made*." So the poet sent a copy of *Leaves of Grass* to the older writer. "I greet you at the beginning of a great career," Emerson graciously replied. But though *Leaves of Grass* didn't sell—reviewers called its twelve poems and preface a "moral cesspool"—Whitman was undeterred and the next year placed Emerson's endorsement on the spine of an expanded edition of *Leaves of Grass* in gold leaf. As if that weren't enough, inside the volume he printed Emerson's letter in its entirety. (He had also released it to the *New York Tribune*.) He then dashed off a couple of anonymous reviews—in praise of himself and his verse: "No sniveller, or tea-drinking poet, no puny clawback or prude, is Walt Whitman. He will bring poems fit to fill the days and nights—fit for men and women with the attributes of throbbing blood and flesh. The body, he teaches, is beautiful. Sex is also beautiful."

Another original poet, who likewise refreshed the language—although unlike Whitman, by compacting it—Emily Dickinson claimed never to have read Whitman, whom she'd heard was scandalous.

"The author is a sort of Emerson run wild," a critic grasped, "glorious, graphic, sublime, ridiculous, spiritual, sensual, great, powerful, savage, tender, sweet, and filthy." It was true. Whitman was all those things, unabashedly: a self-promoter, an egotist, and a poet who would brazenly take his own measure. By the third and expanded edition of *Leaves of Grass* (1860), the eroticism of the poetry was unmistakable: the poet's love of men and his love of women, and the celebration of same-sex love and of auto-eroticism. "Copulation is no more rank to me than death is," he writes. Embarrassed, Emerson suggested Whitman tone it down. Part Barnum and part Rabelais, Whitman would do no such thing. Five years later, when Whitman's boss, Interior Secretary James Harlan, found a copy of *Leaves of Grass*, which he considered obscene (for some reason Harlan had been rummaging through Whitman's desk), he fired the poet on the spot. Whitman soldiered on.

He continued to write poems that do not date or fade, beloved and haunting poems like the early and exultant "Song of Myself" or the elegiac tribute to Abraham Lincoln, "When Lilacs Last in the Dooryard Bloom'd." There are poems of the present and future, like "Crossing Brooklyn Ferry"; poems of the sexual, like the homoerotic "Calamus" poems; or poems of war and empathy, such as "Vigil Strange I Kept on the Field One Night" in *Drum-Taps*, which was written during the Civil War. He revised and republished *Leaves of Grass*, rearranging the poems' order of appearance and tweaking their titles, adding and subtracting, varying his vocabulary, shifting emphasis. In doing so, he became the poet of change as well as the poet of humanity and hope—in spite of the ruthless getting and spending that had begun to characterize an America "saturated in corruption, bribery, falsehood, mal-administration," as Whitman would write of the Gilded Age, shaking a shaggy head. "The men believe not in the women," Whitman lamented, "nor the women in the men." But he remained the poet of belief when there was little or none. "I am a man who has perfect faith," he said early and late. "The faith that never balks."

Of course we know—or sense—that at times he protests too much. For Whitman is also a poet of longing as much as fulfilment. "I perceive I have not really understood any thing, not a single object, and that no man ever can," he writes in "As I Ebb'd with the Ocean of Life." Not a poet of facile optimism, Whitman is a poet of desire: for a better world, a better self, a fuller future. That's perhaps what keeps us near to him—his willingness to see through the dark.

It had been harder to maintain faith during the Civil War. In 1862, Whitman had rushed to Washington in search of his younger brother, First Lieutenant George Whitman of the 51st New York Infantry, who had been wounded, although not badly, at the horrific battle of Fredericksburg. After Whitman found George, he decided to stay in Washington, and though soon fired from the Interior Department, Whitman quickly found employment in the attorney general's office. But Whitman's good friend and fellow writer William O'Connor was so incensed by Whitman's dismissal that he took up the lance for Whitman, whom he promoted as the "good gray poet."

By then, Whitman's hair had indeed turned white, and if not quite a renegade any longer, he remained a maverick whose tall, broad frame was easily identified on the streets of Washington. "Locks profuse and white, eyes big and blue, cheeks ruddy, throat bare, wide collar turned back, slouched felt hat punched in," the journalist Mary Clemmer Ames described Whitman, "a perfect lion apparently in muscle and vitality—this is Walt Whitman. Every sunshiny day he 'loafs' and invites his soul on the Avenue." Writer John Burroughs, also working for government agencies, was likewise enamored with "glorious old Walt," whom he accompanied on long leisurely walks beyond the city, talking of immortality and the soul.

Born in Huntington, New York, to a Quaker family—Dutch on his mother's side—for many years Whitman relished the bustling, growing, tumbling, honking cities of Brooklyn and New York. He dropped out of school early, worked as a teacher, a carpenter, a typesetter, and a printer, and he edited and wrote for the Democratic papers the *Aurora* and then the *Brooklyn Daily Eagle*. As a typesetter and printer, he actually handled words—little shards of the alphabet on the printer's table; touch becomes an important metaphor in his work: the tactile and sensual become ways of knowing the world. In 1848, he traveled South with one of his brothers; there, Whitman briefly wrote in New Orleans for the paper *The Crescent* before returning to Brooklyn, where he began a weekly newspaper, also Democratic but antislavery, known as the *Freeman*.

But, as Emerson said after receiving *Leaves of Grass*, Whitman's career "must have had a long foreground somewhere, for such a start." Though Whitman cited Thomas Paine and the Quaker Elias Hicks as intellectual forebears, no one quite knows where and how he decided to write with what he called "an American rude tongue." Certainly the confounding *Leaves of Grass* caught the rush and flow of young America, its democratic vistas and open plains, its buzz of professions and people, its hounded slaves and trained sopranos, its racial divisions and acrimonies as well as its slang and the sheer beauty of utterance for utterance sake.

For though he savored untrodden paths and the open road, Whitman was also the poet of the city. He loved New York. "New York's the place!" he told Traubel. "If you wish the profound, generous, encompassing things, New York is your natural center of gravity," he exclaimed. In 1881, in the sixth edition of *Leaves of Grass*, he was calling himself "Walt Whitman, a kosmos, of Manhattan the son." He roamed city streets and ambled along the dilapidated wharves, and from the twenty-five-cent balcony seats, he devoured the large gestures of such tragedians as Junius Brutus Booth or Fanny Kemble; he attended the opera as often as possible, relishing in particular the voice of Marietta Alboni, from whom he learned that the voice can itself be an instrument.

Yet Whitman adored Washington too. "I was always between two loves at that time," he explained to Traubel. "I wanted to be in New York, I had to be in Washington: I was never in the one place but I was restless for the other: my heart was distracted." Washington offered fine scenery, "plenty of hills, and a noble river," he said. And there Whitman had met the handsome young horsecar conductor Peter Doyle, an Irish native raised in the South and recently a soldier in the Confederate army; he and Whitman were intimate, loving companions until 1873, when Whitman left Washington.

Whitman had also tended the wounded Union and Confederate soldiers in the regimental, brigade, and division hospitals, which were often just tents on a cracked field where the injured men on the frozen ground were "lucky," Whitman said, "if their blanket is spread on a layer of pine or hemlock twigs." Some of the boys, he recalled, were no more than sixteen. In the district hospitals, as a "wound-dresser," he mopped feverish brows, read to the soldiers, wrote their letters home, and tried to cheer them with little gifts, such as apples, oranges, or sweet crackers. Later, he claimed he'd wrecked his own health with the constant care and sorrow of it all. But, as he also told Traubel, he wouldn't have done otherwise.

———

Nor would Horace Traubel. His devotion to Walt Whitman was complete and lifelong. Part acolyte, part sympathetic confidant, and part son, Traubel was a kind man who has more or less disappeared from view except for his attachment to Whitman. And yet by the time of Traubel's death in 1919—the centenary of Whitman's birth—many of Traubel's writings had been translated into German, French, and Japanese; he was known in America and abroad as a committed socialist, a committed humanitarian, and what Helen Keller called a champion "of liberty, of manhood and womanhood, of justice and righteousness." Eugene Debs said of Traubel that he "has the clear vision of a prophet, the analytical mind of a philosopher, the heroic soul of a martyr, and the unpolluted heart of a child."

The son of Jewish German immigrant lithographer Maurice Traubel and of Katherine Grunder, who was not Jewish, Traubel briefly worked for his father though he had literary aspirations, and while a bank clerk in Philadelphia, he served as that city's correspondent to the Boston *Commonwealth*, contributing hundreds of pieces, mainly on political topics such as women's rights and race relations. He also wrote editorials and small literary reviews for other papers, helped establish a speakers' club where topics ranged from Arctic explorations to copyright law, and was instrumental in the founding of the Philadelphia Society for Ethical Culture. In 1890, he launched the journal *The Conservator* to foster communication among liberal groups, and in 1904 he gathered forty of his own prose poems in a derivative volume called *Chants Communal*—no doubt a tribute to Whitman's "Chants Democratic"—that intended to inspire working people and plead for inclusiveness, equality, and love.

Yet it's for his devotion to Walt Whitman that we recognize Traubel's name. Each day for four years, Traubel would copy down Whitman's conversation on scraps of papers, stuff them in his pockets, and then, to keep them fresh, transcribe them immediately on returning home. So when he published the first volume of *With Walt Whitman in Camden*, he opted for completeness over selection. Likely Traubel was after something like Whitman's own poetry. "Do I contain multitudes? Very well then I contain multitudes."

The first volume of Traubel's undertaking sold poorly, and poor sales endangered the existence of a second volume. But *With Walt Whitman in Camden*, volume two, did appear in 1908, with a different publisher. Unfortunately, it tried the patience of many a critic, precisely because it was Whitman unedited, which meant loaded with big chunks of repetitive, irrelevant, and tedious material, often about housekeeping matters or which of the various pictures of Whitman looked most like him. The fawning of his friends, the inclusion of laudatory correspondence, and the trivial and digressive nature of the conversations often muffled Whitman's far more cogent remarks on writing and writers or on his war experiences. "One volume of Horace Traubel's shirt-sleeve Boswellianism was tolerable, even valuable," said a reviewer. "A second volume of 563 closely printed pages is too much." Still, Traubel had offered an invaluable gift to literary historians, scholars, biographers, and Whitman fans—of that there could be no doubt—by supplying them with a rich resource that would be mined for years and years to come.

And Traubel kept at it. While preparing another book of his own poems, he worked on a third volume of Whitman's conversation, which covered just the years 1888 to 1889. It appeared in 1914, this time published by Mitchell Kennerley, who also published Edna St. Vincent Millay, Walter Lippmann, and the American edition of D. H. Lawrence's *Sons and Lovers*. It was the last volume to appear in Traubel's lifetime.

For with his finances precarious, his travels and writing incessant, and some of his friends sent to prison for protesting America's involvement in World War I, which he deplored, an exhausted Traubel suffered two mild heart attacks and a minor stroke. Once robust, his health continued to deteriorate, and in the fall of 1919, Horace Traubel died, for he said he'd heard Walt Whitman calling.

Traubel had been working on the fourth volume of *Walt Whitman in Camden*, which wasn't published until 1953, when it was edited by the Whitman scholar Sculley Bradley; in 1964, volume five appeared, edited by Gertrude Traubel, Traubel's daughter, but the sixth installment of conversations, which she had also worked on, didn't appear until 1982, and the seventh in 1992. In all, there were nine huge volumes—the last two were not published until 1996. The sum total is extraordinary: an invaluable compendium of observations, insights, overtures, obsessions, and empathy from "an outdoors man," as Whitman said, "serving an indoor sentence."

But the fact remains that the material begs for compression. The nine bulky volumes of Traubel's transcriptions are cumbersome, redundant and taxing even for the most ardent Whitman admirer. As a result, the material is neither well-known nor easily accessible. Thus, in choosing selections for what is essentially a table-talk edition of Whitman's reflections, I have followed Traubel's lead: I decontextualized Whitman, which is to say, I excluded Traubel's voice and his occasional interruptions or asides. (Other editors of the conversations did not.) And more importantly, I have chosen to arrange Whitman's musings in categories familiar to the general reader, omitting commentary on local Camden weather, Camden politics, free trade, money matters, or the negotiations for his tomb at Harleigh Cemetery. Similarly, I excluded discussion of the temperature in his room (too hot), his ailments, and the back-and-forth with obsequious disciples. Some of this material may be important for scholars, but for the general reader I've tried to select the frequently recurring pronouncements, whether about nature, his poetry, art, or about other writers that can stand alone or, better yet, provide for the reader the good company that Whitman generously afforded me.

For I found him to be a remarkable man, alert and engaged and without regret, a democrat in all things although not without his prejudices. He firmly believed in the freedoms that rightfully belong to every person but had never been an abolitionist (he distrusted radicalism of every kind); and fallible, he could not fully embrace racial equality. Yet, in reading through his observations and declarations, I believe now more than ever that Walt Whitman remains an original, a man far ahead of his time who insisted on being himself. Proud never to have backed down or away from what he wanted to do, he did not mask his own wish, even his burning need, to be recognized. So he collaborated with Horace Traubel, and hence with me, and with all of us who can for a little while eavesdrop on Whitman speaking about Whitman and his work, about other poets, about critics, about religion, and about his beloved America. And as he speaks of life and death and the cosmos, he again bids us today, as he has always done, *"Be of good cheer, we will / not desert you."*

"Now, to you, as we sit here, face to face."

Nature

*If a man starts out for an instant to get something better
than nature, then I say, God help him!*

Nature has a keen way of putting its strength out: if a man
lack in one sense, nature puts the strength—the strength
due that—into another.

———

We carry our fresh air with us, wherever we go. He who
has it, has it anywhere—nothing can rob him of it.

———

I find in all characters that live close to nature, capri-
ciousness, variability—they seem to pattern after nature's
higher rules. The children are that way, and dogs, cats—
not but that their perceptions, intuitions, are keen enough,
but with the capricious, too.

———

Nature follows close upon the mood of the mind that
contemplates her—is moody as it is moody, bright as it is
bright, laughs in its laughter, weeps in its tears.

———

Our human nature is like the weather—it comes from all quarters—and while all these suggestions, reforms, doctrines, may help, certainly belong, no one of them can do the business for us. It is too long a story.

———

I know best of all the rivers—the grand, sweeping, curving, gently undulating rivers. Oh! the memories of rivers—the Hudson—the Ohio—the Mississippi! It would be hard to put into a word the charms of the Mississippi: they are distinctive, undoubted—do not consist in what is called beauty—which, for instance, would be picked out as essentially the wonders of the Hudson—consist rather in amplitude, power, force,—a lazy muddy water-course, immense in sweep—in its various wanderings. The Hudson is quite another critter—the neatest, sweetest, most delicate, clearest, cleanest river in the world. Not sluttish—not a trace of it and I think I am pretty familiar with it—at least as it was—for the matter of 200 miles or so, which is about the whole story. The beginnings of the Delaware are scattered all through southern New York—delicate threads finally making way to union and power. Rivers! Oh the rivers!

———

Have you ever thought how much is in the negative quality of nature—the negative—the simply loafing, doing nothing, worrying about nothing, living out of doors and getting fresh air, plenty of sleep—letting everything else take care of itself?

———

I think our people are getting entirely too decent. They like nice white hands, men and women. They are too much disturbed by dirt. They need the open air, coarse work—physical tasks: something to do away from the washstand and the bathtub. God knows, I'm not opposed to clean hands. But clean hands, too, may be a disgrace.

———

We seem afraid of the natural forces. John Burroughs puts it well, says, if the American is only dry, he is not content to take a drink of pure cold water, but must put sugar into it, or a flavor. To me, these things—the things of which these are the type—are the prominent dangers in the future of our America.

———

The exhilaration of such freedom—the going and coming—the being master of yourself and of the road! No one who is not a walker can begin to know it!

———

Oh! the long, long walks, way into the nights!—in the after hours—sometimes lasting till two or three in the

morning! The air, the stars, the moon, the water—what a
fullness of inspiration they imparted!—what exhilaration!
And there were the detours, too—wanderings off into
the country out of the beaten path: I remember one place
in Maryland in particular to which we would go. How
splendid, above all, was the moon—the full moon, the half
moon: and then the wonder, the delight, of the silences.

———

There was a book published some years ago called *The
Night Side of Nature*—I have often thought, if there was
not a night side of human character, too—of literature—
of personality—a sort of phantasmagoric *delirium tremens*.

———

It is almost incredible what a little stretch of nature will
do to arouse a fellow—convert him, so to speak. I cannot think of a rarer experience than one I met on the
river Saguenay, up there in Canada. The river's water is
an inky black—a curious study, I believe, to this day to
the scientific men: take it up in a bucket, and it is still
unmistakably black—the color of the stream. Oh! that
great day! Down the stream a boat—sails open—wing-
a-wing—one one side, one the other—patched, stained,
heavy—but oh! how beautiful! It was a curious revelation
out of little means. Wing-a-wing is rarely fine anyhow—I
have not known it much in pictures—but few artists can
accomplish it. See then, the large result of what may seem

a small impulse. Why should we go hunt beauty then—I should rather ask—where can you go to get away from it?

————◆————

Nature only gives us a little of her territory, her domain—and retains the rest: retains it for her own modesties, for reasons of her own. These other fellows—the orthodox—call that *waste*—but no, it is something else—something *far* else. And out of this principle—these recognitions—came *Leaves of Grass*. And it, I, must be, are, more indebted to nature than we know.

————◆————

I have aimed to draw, or remain, near the mysteries of nature: near them, to feel their breath, even when I knew nothing of what they meant, and could but wonder and listen, as if to vague music. I had all this clear from the start—I had all these determinations—I never erred—never strayed. And now, whether to be charged as a fool, or as reckoned victor, I am sure my choice, at least for me, was well-taken—was, finally, the only path possible for me to foot.

The Human Heart

I should like to know, what is life?
Yes indeed—what is life?

There's something in the human critter which only needs to be nudged to reveal itself: something inestimably eloquent, precious: not always observed: it is a folded leaf: not absent because we fail to see it: the right man comes—the right hour; the leaf is lifted.

———

The largest part of our human tragedies are humanly avoidable: they come from greed, from carelessness, from causes not catastrophic, elemental: with more radical good heart most of our woes would disappear.

———

It is my opinion that the great affairs of our time (perhaps of any time—certainly of ours) go their way, revolutionize things, re-make, re-form, away, apart from, all churches, societies, liberalizations of any sort; that beneath all the surface-shows are influences—great undertows—through which the world is pressed on and on. Not by cries of priests or tabernacles, but in the human heart.

———

The important thing to us now is the life here—the people here: yes, that's the important immediate thing: the earth struggle—our effort, our task, here to build up our human social body into finer results: the daily hourly job right here, right now: yours, mine: the rest will come—the beyond: we are not called upon to bother about it at once: it would only confuse matters: we can make our declaration about it, say our yes, then stop: our responsibilities are on the earth.

Writing

*The trick of literary style! I almost wonder if it is
not chiefly having no style at all.*

I take it there are qualities—latent forces—in all men
which need to be shaken up into life: to shake them up—
that is the function of the writer.

———

The idea must always come first—is indispensable. Take
my own method—if you call it that. I have the idea clearly
and fully realized before I attempt to express it. Then I let
it go. The idea becomes so important to me I may perhaps
underrate the other element—the expressional element—
that first, last and all the time emphasis placed by literary
men on the mere implement of words instead of upon the
work itself. You see it in Doctor Johnson—expression
always paramount.

———

If a fellow is to write poetry the secret is—get in touch
with humanity—know what the people are thinking
about: retire to the very deepest sources of life—back,
back, till there is no further point to retire to.

———

The secret of it all is, to write in the gush, the throb, the flood, of the moment—to put things down without deliberation—without worrying about their style—without waiting for a fit time or place. I always worked that way. I took the first scrap of paper, the first doorstep, the first desk, and wrote—wrote, wrote. No prepared picture, no elaborated poem, no after-narrative, could be what the thing itself is. You want to catch its first spirit—to tally its birth. By writing at the instant the very heart-beat of life is caught.

———

I suppose every man has his purposes. I had mine—to have no purpose—to state, to capture, the drift of a life— to let things flow in, one after another, take their places, their own way.

———

It is right to cut out, put in, prune, change, to your heart's content—but God help you if the world detects you at it! To the world a poem must each time be a new discovery— not seem old, stale, *made*. Everything depends on that—to not make anything of the labor obvious.

———

Writers write for exercise—determine what they should write—therefore do. Would never think of writing as the trees put forth their green—as men fall in love—perforce—because there is no other thing to do.

———

I don't seem to have any advice to give, except perhaps this: Be natural, be natural, be natural! Be a damned fool, be wise if you must (can't help it), be anything—only be natural! Almost any writer who is willing to be himself will amount to something—because we all amount to something, to about the same thing, at the roots. The trouble mostly is that writers become writers and cease to be men: writers reflect writers, writers again reflect writers, until the man is worn thin—worn through.

———

When you write do you take anybody's advice about writing? Don't do it: nothing will so mix you up as advice. If a fellow wants to keep clear about himself he must first of all swear a big oath that he'll never take any advice.

———

Every man has to learn his own best method: my method is to go slow, extra slow. All great work is cautious work—is done with an eye on all the horizons of the spirit: in the absence of such gravity we become dabblers—the big things don't get said, don't get done.

———

The point is, not to prove your possession of a style, but to move the people along the line of their nobler impulses. The style will readily enough accommodate itself. Napoleon didn't study rules first: he first of all studied his task. And there was Lincoln, too: see how he went his own lonely road, disregarding all the usual ways—refusing the guides, accepting no warnings: just keeping his appointment with himself every time. I can hear the advisers saying scornful things to him. They offered him ready-made methods. But Lincoln would only retort: "I want that battle fought—I want that battle won: I don't care how or when: but fought and won!"

———

It's not quite the thing to take language by the throat and make it yield you beautiful results. I don't want beautiful results—I want results: honest results: expression: expression.

———

Perfect English and perfect sense don't always go together!

———

The surprise to me is, how much is spontaneously suggested which a man could never have planned for. I sit down to write: one seemingly simple idea brings into view a dozen others: so my work grows. A writer can do nothing for men more necessary, satisfying, than just simply to reveal to them the infinite possibilities of their own souls.

———

A man makes a pair of shoes—the best—he expects nothing of it: he knows they will wear out: that's the end of the good shoe, the good man. Any kind of a scribbler writes any kind of a poem and expects it to last forever. Yet the poems wear out, too—often faster than the shoes. I don't know but in the long run almost as many shoes as poems last out the experience—we put the shoes into museums, we put the poems into books.

———

In all imaginative work, all pure poetic work, there must especially come in a primal quality, not to be mentioned, named, described, but always felt when present: the direct off-throwing of nature, parting the ways between formal, conventional, borrowed expression and the fervor of genuine spirit.

———

Breaking loose is the thing to do: breaking loose, resenting the bonds, opening new ways: but when a fellow breaks loose or starts to or even only thinks he thinks he'll revolt he should be quite sure he knows what he has undertaken. I expected hell: I got it: nothing that has occurred to me was a surprise: there probably is still more to come: that will not surprise me, either.

———

The great French writer Legouvé says this is the final, the supreme, test, after all else is tried—how will a poem read, recite, deliver: with what effect? How will it hold its own when repeated? That is the court in which it must justify itself.

———

Beware of the literary cliques—keep well in the general crowd: beware of book sympathies, caste sympathies. Some one said here the other day—who was it?—"Mr. Whitman you seem to have sympathy for manhood but not for authorship?" It seems to me that all real authorship is manhood—that my sympathy for manhood includes authorship even if it don't make authorship a preferred object of worship. What is authorship in itself if you cart it away from the main stream of life? It is starved, starved: it is a dead limb off the tree—it is the unquickened seed in the ground.

———

Don't most men who write write without knowing life? Write all over the surface of the earth, never dig a foot into the ground—everlastingly write.

Writers

Some day I'll die—maybe surprise you all by a sudden disappearance: then where'll my book be? That's the one thing that excites me: most authors have the same dread—the dread that something or other essential that they have written may somehow become side-tracked, lost—lost forever.

William Shakespeare

Do you suppose I accept the almost luny worship of Shakespeare—the cult worship, the college-chair worship? Not a bit of it—not a bit of it. I do not think Shakespeare was the all in all of literature. I think there were twenty thousand things coming before him and at his time and since—things, men, illuminati—and everything has to be counted. Shakespeare was the greatest of his kind—but how about his kind?

———

If Shakespeare had any weakness, it was in his women. All his women are fashioned so: in King John, in Richard—everywhere—the product of feudalism—daintily, delicately fashioned. Yet I suppose all right, occupying a fit position—in themselves a reflex of their times, though to us, to our eyes, open to criticism.

———

Only one Shakespeare for forever to forever. To me that is rank nonsense—it leads to imbecility. Yet it may be a safety valve. Some people need harmless enthusiasms: better zest, ardor, warmth, decision, then nothing—than merely colorless inanity: better misapplied heat than no heat at all. But for any philosophic mind—for anyone capable of perspective, of seeing back and forward, of measuring here and beyond—the Shakespeare worship is poor business enough—poor business enough.

———

Shakespeare shows undoubted defects: he often uses a hundred words where a dozen would do: it is true that there are many pithy terse sentences everywhere: but there are countless prolixities: though as for the overabundances of words more might be said: as, for instance, that he was not ignorantly prolific: that he was like nature itself: nature, with her trees, the oceans: nature, saying "there's lots of this, infinitudes of it—therefore, why spare it? If you ask for ten I give you a hundred, for a hundred I give you a thousand, for a thousand I give you ten thousand." It may be that we should look at it in that way: not complain of it: rather understand its amazing intimations.

———

I should not like to go on record as picking flaws in Shake-speare—as standing in the attitude of critic, questioner—for that would be unjust to me. And not, besides, be square with my known principles, for, as with Emerson, I claim Shakespeare for the top—as the justification of many things but for them questioned. Nor do I know but Shake-speare after all leveled his lances—some of his lances—low enough—against many things we are against.

———

Shakespeare, Browning, unexpressibly grand as their work has been, are democrats rebellious against democracy—not made for this era, stage, America—answering other conditions, answering them well, but with something of hautcur towards common ways of average men—which is in fact America. I know it is small, carping, unworthy, to offer any word of criticism of a man like Shakespeare, who has done so much towards the richening of literature, of man—who was a luminary of the first order—perhaps the first in the first. And so I grant all that—yield it all. Only protest that these centuries of annotations have not suc-ceeded in making Shakespeare answer to the modern—the democratic modern. And what I say of Shakespeare I always feel about Goethe, too. And I know, moreover, that some of the noblest of us all have stood reactionary on that question of democracy—of man in the average—the vital moving mass.

———

Goethe suggests books—carries the aroma of books about with him—seems to be a great man with books, by books, from books. Now, whatever Shakespeare was or was not, he was not that sort of man: he came, with all his scholarship, direct from nature. To me that means oh! so much: to come straight from life—to be rooted in an immediate fact.

———

People don't dare face the fact Shakespeare. They are all tied to a fiction that is called Shakespeare—a Shakespearean illusion.

———

It's very difficult to talk about Shakespeare in a frank vein: there's always somebody about with a terrific prejudice to howl you down.

John Milton

It seems to me that Milton is a copy of a copy—not only Homer but the *Aeneid*: a sort of modern repetition of the same old story: legions of angels, devils: war is declared: waged, moreover, even as a story it enlists little of my attention: he seems to me like a bird—soaring yet overweighted: dragged down, as if burdened—too greatly burdened: a lamb in its beak: its flight not graceful, powerful, beautiful, satisfying, like the gulls we see over the Delaware in midwinter—their simple notion a delight—attracting you when they first break upon your sight: soaring, soaring, irrespective of cold or storm. It is true, Milton soars, but with dull, unwieldy motion.

Samuel Johnson

Dr. Johnson, it is plain, is not our man: he belongs to a past age: comes to us with the odor, the sound, the taste, the appearance, of great libraries, musty books, old manuscripts. My chief complaint against Johnson is that he lacks veracity: lacks the veracity which we have the right to exact from any man—most of all from the writer, the recorder, the poet. Johnson never cared as much to meet men—learn from men—as to drive them down roughshod—to crowd them out—to crush them against the wall. He is a type of the smart man—a ponderous type: of the man who says the first thing that comes—who does anything to score a point—who is not concerned for truth but to make an impression.

James Boswell

The more I see of the book [*Life of Johnson*] the more I realize what a roaring bull the Doctor was and what a braying ass Boswell was.

Voltaire

Voltaire, after the intellectual sinuosities, deep down, down, to bottom truths, was triumphantly on our side. A wonderful force—his anger persistent, mighty—as when after some priesthood, how he clutched, swore, persisted, indignation deepening in him down to the very joints of his toes. There is a sense in which he is ours, a sense in which we would after all say he was *not*: but, as I have said, get past the intellectual sinuosities: then your way is clear.

Voltaire and Jean-Jacques Rousseau

There were some people in the old days—in my youth—early years (some of the freethinkers, some scholars) who looked upon Voltaire, well, I suppose as about the best salt of the earth—the greatest man so far, beyond all odds. And not fools either—wise men—noble fellows—big, devoted, clear-eyed. But whether or no, Voltaire is a vital breathing force in all our modern life—a majestic great figure, set up in the eyes of history—yes, in man's heart, even. And who could measure what he has meant for America, even—freedom? One of the subtlest men, too, in all time, any land—wise not only in what he did do, but wisest in what he did not do. Able in all the difficulties of that period to steer a safe path—to keep power, protection, on his side—to baffle enemies—oh! the worst enemies!—to meet dagger with more than dagger: science, art, the buttress of philosophy. Oh! Cute as a modern Yankee! Great for France—great for the world! Able to cope with the damnablest foes—to damn them all. I can see no more *necessary* figure in all history. He brought gifts, courage, insight, the like—and won a new world by them—remade Europe, made America. Did you ever read accounts of his triumphant entry into Paris that last year or so of his life? It is one of the most instructive recitals possible. I never forget it. Power several times got him—seized him. He had been in the Bastille, suffered banishment, all that, but was never without friends—heroic, influential friends. And in that last year went back to Paris. Oh! What a triumph! The very elite of the then world—fashionable, intellectual, brilliant Paris, all at his feet—nobility, populace—the proudest bending low to this old man. The throne—the king at that time (who was he?)—turned the thing over—determined not to recognize Voltaire. So it was understood there was to be no reception at court, which was enough to fire the pile—to bring out every latent factor of adoration—noble, people, savant, all. Indeed, so wild the demonstration that in spite of the old man—half mad, half happy—frowns, smile mixing—his horses were unharnessed from the carriage—he dragged in more than state (what state was ever like that?)—king, malcontents stupefied. The old man was *very* old then—yet master of the situation. But a few months after, died. Curiously, Rousseau died about that same time—a little later, I think—with*out* reception—poor, in poverty, neglected—taken care of by the charity of some pitying noblemen. Rousseau—that other giant! And, Horace, did you ever think deeply, determinedly, of the significance of these two lives? Oh! The stream runs very deep! There is a wise man somewhere who sums up this way: Voltaire, says he, moved kings, priests—toppled over false honors, thrones—brought men back to external realities; Rousseau moved their hearts and minds—souls. And God knows who greatest! Which matters little.

Robert Burns

The average critic bases all he knows, says, thinks, of Burns, on two or three or four poems—on "The Cotter's Saturday Night," "Tam O'Shanter," "The Twa Dogs," "The Twa Brigs"—some of which will answer the tests, standards, they bring to measure them. The real Burns was the Burns of out-of-doors, frolicking, drinking, farming, ploughing the fields—of women—of poverty—of struggle: the Burns we see in the letters, for instance— those incomparable, heart-given letters—and of all this these fellows make little account, if they even know.

Heinrich Heine

Heine! Oh how great! The more you stop to look, to examine, the deeper seem the roots, the broader and higher the umbrage. And Heine was free—was one of the men who win by degrees. He was the master of a pregnant sarcasm: he brought down a hundred humbuggeries if he brought down two. At times he plays with you with a deliberate, baffling sportiveness.

———

Heine was always warm, pulsing—his style pure, lofty, sweeping, in its wild strength. Heine knew more than

Burns. It becomes a familiar reproach to speak of Heine's "mockery." It does not disturb me: I never find myself shocked, repelled, by it. They call it "mockery": I think there should be another word for it—that there is, though I can't recall it now: for Heine deserves a better word. They may call it a trick with Heine: a trick: but whatever it be called it is very effective. It seems to belong honestly to Heine—is quite in its place in him: is not an importation.

Johann Wolfgang von Goethe

Goethe impresses me as above all to stand for essential literature, art, life—to argue the importance of centering life in self—in perfect persons—perfect you, me: to force the real into the abstract ideal: to make himself, Goethe, the supremest example of personal identity: everything making for it: in us, in Goethe: every man repeating the same experience.

Goethe lived in a little slip of a place—a little town interested in small wares—given up to petty, trivial gossipings: yet he glorified himself, glorified the place, by his tremendous vital grasp of eternal principles—by the infinite reach of his faculty—his illimitable intuitions.

Sir Walter Scott

Scott was the great troubadour—the singer—tremendous in fire (almost fury). I can see him—see the castle—the processions of ladies—the grand dames—robes—color—

gaiety—Scott ahead—the minstrel. O yes! I can hear his songs—voice—the cadence—the stir—listeners. All fresh, a new day. Scott will always be that for *me*. And for the world? Well, the world will never lose sight of him.

James Fenimore Cooper

Cooper was always an outdoor influence: he is perennial fresh air, pure seas; a living accuser of our civilization. Our civilization is anyhow a morbid one—introspective, consciously sinful. But Cooper maintained his independence, manhood, from the very first. *The Spy*, all the sea tales, Long Tom Coffin—what a creation that! Cooper was fiery, I suppose from a very young man, up to the last, yet generous, large, free, exciting respect everywhere. Used to servants, rich, served. Yes, a truly vigorous physiog, too: a sea-dog's face—yet more than that.

———

Cooper was a curious paradox—very hard to deal with— possessing great shining qualities—some harsh ones, too—perhaps in the direction of a too severe individualism if that can be; but breathing the open airs—never, never the odor of libraries! The life of Cooper has not yet been written. The time will come for it, without question. Cooper was one of the first-raters—had a vein of asperity which sort of cut him loose from the literary classes—perhaps preserved him—who knows?

William Blake
Blake began and ended in Blake.

Percy Bysshe Shelley
I have a warm place even for Shelley. He seems so opposite—so ethereal—all ethereal—always living in the presence of a great ideal, as I do not. He was not sensual—he was not even sensuous.

John Keats and Lord Byron
Keats' whole being seemed absorbed in what is called beauty—the sense of the beautiful —perfection of form—polish—aesthetic beauty. It was on him, on this, the criticism fell. It was vitriol. On Keats, Byron, Kirke White, others, this scurrility, abuse, contempt, was bestowed. Byron prospered under it—indeed, I don't know but that was the greatest factor in his development. He published his first book at 19 or 20 or 21, thereabouts—*Hours of Idleness*— and very good ones, some, too. But it was left for the later experience to make him what he is now known to have been.

Edgar Allan Poe
Do I like Poe? At the start, for many years, not: but three or four years ago I got to reading him again, reading and liking, until at last—yes, now—I feel almost convinced that he is a star of considerable magnitude, if not a sun, in

the literary firmament. Poe was morbid, shadowy, lugu-brious—he seemed to suggest dark nights, horrors, spec-tralities—I could not originally stomach him at all. But today I see more of him than that—much more. If that was all there was to him he would have died long ago. I was a young man of about thirty, living in New York, when "The Raven" appeared—created its stir: everybody was excited about it—every reading body: somehow it did not enthuse me.

William Cullen Bryant

Of all Americans so far, I am inclined to rank Bryant highest. Bryant has all that was knotty, gnarled, in Dante, Carlyle: besides that, has great other qualities. It has always seemed to me Bryant, more than any other American, had the power to suck in the air of spring, to put it into his song, to breathe it forth again—the palpable influence of spring: the new entrance to life. A feature in Bryant which is never to be under-weighed is the marvelous purity of his work in verse. It was severe—oh! so severe!—never a waste word—the last superfluity struck off: a clear name-less beauty pervading and overarching all the work of his pen. Bryant the man I met often—often. He was not much of a talker, would not impress or attract as such. His voice was a good one—not deep—not fascinating—not moving, eloquent. Bryant tried lecturing. He was a great homeopathist—a great Unitarian: at the time of the homeopathic excitement he delivered two or three lectures on the subject. But I don't think he liked lecturing himself, and he did not prove a success with others. He was an American: that is one of the palpable facts: thoroughly American, patriotic: moreover, he had a tint of the Scotch left—a trifle hypochondriac—a bit irascible. I have often observed marked traces running through the Scotch character of general hypochrondriacism: Burns? yes: and Carlyle. Bryant bore the marks of it. I know it is not invariable: there are exceptions: but in the main its existence cannot be questioned.

———

Bryant was trained in the classics—made no departures. He was a healthy influence—was not a closet man: belonged out of doors: but he was afraid of my work: he was interested, but afraid: I remember that he always expressed wonder that with what he called my power and gifts and essential underlying respect for beauty I refused to accept and use the only medium which would give me complete expression. I have often tried to think of myself as writing *Leaves of Grass* in Thanatopsisian verse. Of course I do not intend this as a criticism of Bryant—only as a demurrer to his objection to me: "Thanatopsis" is all right in Thanatopsisian verse: I suppose Bryant would fare as badly in *Leaves of Grass* verse as I would fare in Thanatopsis verse.

John Greenleaf Whittier

Whittier's poetry stands for morality (not its *ensemble* or in any true philosophic sense) but as filter'd through a Puritanical and Quaker filter—is very valuable as a genuine utterance and fine one—with many local and yankee and *genre* bits—all hued with zealous anti-slavery coloring. All the *genre* contributions are precious—all help. Whittier is rather a grand figure—but pretty lean and ascetic.

Henry Wadsworth Longfellow

Longfellow imports all sorts of things into Hiawatha: but did an Indian ever talk so? Was it not the man in the library who was doing the talking?

———

Longfellow was no revolutionaire: never travelled new paths: of course never broke new paths: in fact was a man who shrank from unusual things—from what was highly colored, dynamic, drastic. Longfellow was the expresser of the common themes—of the little songs of the masses— perhaps will always have some vogue among average readers of English. Such a man is always in order—could not be dispensed with—maintains a popular conventional pertinency.

Victor Hugo

I always have looked upon Hugo as a man among the first forces in literature—in the literature of aspiration. Yet *Les*

Miserables has a good deal to do with horror, convicts—hopeless convicts—with that phase of life. It may be that Hugo exalts, toplofticates, the ragamuffins too much. But that is only one side of the question. Hugo cannot be judged simply from one phase of his work.

Nathaniel Hawthorne

I consider Cooper greater—much greater—than Hawthorne, just as I consider Bryant—though the world will not have it so—incomparably greater than Longfellow. But such comparisons, I suppose, are not good, wherever made.

———

I have been reading about Hawthorne tonight. What a devil of a Copperhead he was! I always more or less despise the Copperheads, irrespective of who they are, their fame—what-not: but aside from that, all my tendencies about Hawthorne are towards him—even affectionate, I may say—for his work, what he represented.

Bronson Alcott

Alcott had a lot of queerities—freakishnesses: not vegetarianism—I do not count that—but transcendental mummeries—worst of all a most vociferous contempt for the body, which I, of course, opposed.

———

Alcott was childlike: he was one of the divine simples; he belonged to the race of the teachers—the peripatetics: the wise wondering seers, instructors: a quite exceptional class of men who in another age, in another country, where such things are more directly popularly cherished and taken pride in, would be set to work at the expense of the state to conduct their schools.

Ralph Waldo Emerson

Emerson's face always seemed to me so clean—as if God had just washed it off. When you looked at Emerson it never occurred to you that there could be any villainies in the world.

———

Emerson was a clear instance of the careful talker. His characteristic feature was being toned down: his invariable manner, wariness—consummate, perfect, prudence—yet not deceit (no—that word don't even come in sight)—an abiding caution as to what he was saying, as if in warning: be in no haste to commit yourself—to say things not justified by your deeper consciousness.

———

There is in some men an indefinable something which flows out and over you like a flood of light—as if they possessed it illimitably—their whole being suffused with it. Being—in fact that is precisely the word. Emerson's whole attitude shed forth such an impression.

———

The wonder is, that Emerson—so delicate—so simple—so fine—should have been heard at all. The significant things are quickly told—that he lived at all—that he worked, wrote—and the world listened. And I always feel of Emerson as I do of Christianity: the acceptance of Christianity was not a credit to Jesus, but to the human race, that it could see, and seeing, welcome; as now with Emerson, the tribute, testimony, not to him but to the modern man, that he can compass so much.

———

Emerson was a most apt, genuine, storyteller: his whole face would light up anticipatingly as he spoke: he was serene, quiet, sweet, conciliating, as a story was coming. Curiously, too, Emerson enjoyed most repeating those stories which told against himself—took off his edge—his own edge: he had a great dread of being egotistic—had a horror of it, if I may say so: a horror—a shrinking from the suspicion of a show of it: indeed, he had a fear of egotism that was almost—who knows, quite?—an egotism itself.

———

It seems to me that out of the cluster of his clusters of merits, greatness, Emerson could best be described by genuineness, absolute frankness, pristine intelligence: as I often say—he is filled with the qualities that go to redeem the whole bookish crew: yes, he redeems them: and we must remember that Emerson was not only spiritual—a creature of dreams, ideals—but knew a thing or two of the earth about him: though he was utterly without guile—utterly, utterly: the most absolutely pure, childlike, while the wisest, creature of our time.

———

Emerson lived according to his lights—not according to libraries, books, literature, the traditions: he was unostentatiously loyal: no collegian, overdone with culture: so gifted, so peculiarly tremendous, that, if I may say so, knowing too much did not as it so often does with the scholar hurt him.

———

Emerson never lacked decision; he was indeed the firmest of men, never shaken from his place—unshockable—he never unhatted to any person or any power—any institution—never went out looking for things which did not come to him of their own accord.

———

I always insist that Emersonism, legitimately followed out, always ends in weakness—takes all color out of life. Not that this could be said of Emerson himself, because, as I point out—as is plain to me—Emerson supplies his own antidote—teaches his own destruction—if seen at his best.

———

The glory of Emerson is that he provides the antidote for Emerson—himself destroys his following.

Henry David Thoreau

Thoreau was a surprising fellow—he is not easily grasped—is elusive: yet he is one of the native forces—stands for a fact, a movement, an upheaval: Thoreau belongs to America, to the transcendental, to the protesters: then he is an outdoor man: all outdoor men everything else being equal appeal to me. Thoreau was not so precious, tender, a personality as Emerson: but he was a force—he looms up bigger and bigger: his dying does not seem to have hurt him a bit: every year has added to his fame. One thing about Thoreau keeps him very near to me: I refer to his lawlessness—his dissent—his going his own absolute road let hell blaze all it chooses.

The great vice in Thoreau's composition was his disdain of the universe—his disdain of cities, companions, civilization.

Thoreau had his own odd ways. Once he got to the house while I was out—went straight to the kitchen where my dear mother was baking some cakes—took the cakes hot from the oven. He was always doing things of the plain sort—without fuss. I liked all that about him.

———

Thoreau had an abstraction about man—a right abstraction: there we agreed. We had our quarrel only on this ground. Yet he was a man you would have to like—an interesting man, simple, conclusive.

James Russell Lowell
Lowell is a palace—plate-glass windows, curtains, prettinesses—built—unexceptionable.

———

Lowell was not a grower—he was a builder. He *built* poems: he didn't put in the seed, and water the seed, and send down his sun—letting the rest take care of itself: he measured his poems—kept them within the formula.

Oliver Wendell Holmes, Sr.
Holmes is no fool—is a man of marked intellect—but nearly always too palpably witty—deliberately so. I think that of all else, deliberate wit is best calculated for failure. Deliberate anything, in fact, the determined starting out to do a thing.

Lafcadio Hearn, George Washington Cable, Sir Walter Scott, James Fenimore Cooper
Hearn has a delicate beautiful nature: he got into instant rapport with the Japanese. These story writers do not as a

rule reach me—I find they stay too much on the surface of the ground. I have tried to read Cable—have read several of his stories—*Madame Delphine* for one, brought here by Logan Smith. They are modelled on the French—show great delicacy, precision, analysis: a capacity for taking up a single act or character—a fragment—and working it out to an extreme individual conclusion, meanwhile missing the law, missing the general atmosphere. I think the American theory would be, should be, must be, something different. My taste has been modelled on another theory— in the school of Scott, of Cooper, of some others of the older writers. How much I am indebted to Scott no one can tell—I couldn't tell it myself—but it has permeated me through and through. If you could reduce the *Leaves* to their elements you would see Scott unmistakably active at the roots. I remember the *Tales of my Landlord, Ivan hoe, The Fortunes of Nigel*—yes, and *Kenilworth*—its great pageantry—then there's *The Heart of Midlothian*, which I have read a dozen times and more. I might say just about the same thing about Cooper, too. He has written books which will survive into the farthest future. Try to think of literature, of the world of boys, today, without Natty Bumppo, *The Spy, The Red Rover*—Oh *The Red Rover*— it used to stir me up clarionlike: I read it many times. Is all this old fashioned? I am not sworn to the old things—not at all—that is, not to old things at the expense of new— but some of the oldest things are the newest. I should not refuse to see and welcome anyone who came to violate the precedents—on the contrary I am looking about for just such men—but a lot of the fresh things are not new—they are only repetitions after all: they do not seem to take life forward but to take it back. I look for the things that take life forward—the new things, the old things, that take life forward. Scott, Cooper, such men, always, perpetually, as a matter of course, always take life forward—take each new generation forward.

Thomas Carlyle

Carlyle was not an apt student of the modern, of literary rebellion—he was raised, imbedded, in older routines. He did not understand humanity—had no faith in humanity, in fact—more than that, he lacked unction: don't you think that's the word to describe it?—he had no religious faith—I am sure he lacked conviction in the triumph of the good. I do not intend to say Carlyle did not contribute—did not do this and that for which humanity will be eternally richer and grateful. What I am trying to say is that he had no avenue of approach to the people; he lost his way in the jungle: the people were not a beautiful abstraction—they were an ugly fact: he shrank from the people. Carlyle was a good deal of a democrat in spite of himself. Carlyle was incapable of seeing men generously, even his friends. One thing Carlyle did understand—the incessant caterwauling of radicals—their unceasing complaints against everything—their inability to appre-

ciate the importance of conservatism, of restraint, even
of persecution.

———————

Carlyle was fed on the pabulum of European libraries: he
learned above all to love strong individualities—men who
would drive on to their ends through whatever obstacles—
men gifted with the genius of extrication—men who were
not particular how they did things but very particular to
have them done. Carlyle had one failing in common with
Thoreau—disdain, contempt, for average human beings:
for the masses of men: he never could understand that
though man was in some ways a devil of a fellow, he was
not all devil or even chiefly devil.

Alfred, Lord Tennyson
Tennyson seems to me the great expression of modern
ennui—the blue devils that afflict modern civilization.
It is the background of every poem—every one of them:
latent there—not always pushed to the front—perhaps
never introduced –but always present, never missed: a
half gloom—even a question—but after all, summed up,
a faith. It is not a note of triumph, but it is there. There
are many to whom life may seem a thing of itself, but the
greatest, noblest, farthest-seeing, largest-hoping of modern
man do not believe this is an endup—this life a closing.

———————

While Tennyson does a good deal of good—oh! incalculable good!—he does harm too—often much harm: his mellifluosity—one may call it: it is great, overwhelming, everything in his imitators is sacrificed to accomplish that.

John Ruskin

Without the railroads, where would our civilization be? Certainly we could ask, where would America be? America in fact could not be. In Ruskin's own corner-lot bit of a country, coaches might still serve, in a way, but in an America—any country continental in its territory, aspirations,—the railroad belongs—has its place. But Ruskin's appeal has its justifications, too. In a time when we are beset everywhere by what is called progress, the spirit of progress, civilization, radicalism, railroads, machinery, it may be well to have men like Carlyle, Ruskin, to strike the alarm—to warn us not to go too far.

Henry James, Sr.

I knew and know very little of this Henry James, but of the father—the old man—I know very much more. I had a friend who was quite intimate with him. So far as I could gather James was the type of the man in his place—in the universities—a man afraid of facts,—divine facts: not to be better expressed than by the figure of a mirror—with its reflection: and the notion of the man who could be very well satisfied with that mirror—but with the fact itself—

oh no! let us not talk about that—hear none of it—would rather be excused!

William Dean Howells and Henry James

The story writers do not as a rule attract me. Howells is more serious—seems to have something to say—James is only feathers to me. What do you make of them?—what is their future significance? Have they any? Don't they just come and go—don't they just skim about, butterfly about, daintily, in fragile literary vessels, for awhile—then bow their way out? They do not deal in elements: they deal only in pieces of things, in fragments broken off, in detached episodes.

Matthew Arnold

Arnold has been writing new things about the United States. Arnold could know nothing about the States—essentially nothing: the real things here—the real dangers as well as the real promises—a man of his sort would always miss. Arnold knows nothing of elements—nothing of things as they start. I know he is a significant figure—I do not propose to wipe him out. He came in at the rear of a procession two thousand years old—the great army of critics, parlor apostles, worshippers of hangings, laces, and so forth and so forth—they never have anything properly at first hand. Naturally I have little inclination their way.

———

What has Arnold contributed for us? Of course I speak of him a good deal with reference to what he said of America —of us—of Emerson. What did he know of us? What value had his divining rod? Sweetness and light? Damn sweetness and light! We have already too much of it! I like the north-west winds—the fearless tides: to brace these— to take these naturally, heroically—as in themselves matters of course! It would seem as if our civilization was doing all it could to get away from all that signified of inherent nativities—of what at best belongs to us all!

Robert Browning

One thing I always feel like saying about Browning—that I am always conscious of his roominess: he is noway a small man: all his connections are big, strong.

Algernon Swinburne

Swinburne either insults you or hugs you—he knows nothing "between": that's just the point—yet that "between" something or other is more worth while than all the rest.

Mark Twain

I have met Clemens, met him many years ago, before he was rich and famous. Like all humorists he was very sober: inclined to talk of the latest things in politics, men, books, a man after old-fashioned models, slow to move, liking to stop and chat—the sort of fellow one is quietly drawn to. Yes, my experience with humorists is, that they are all of the more serious color.

———

I think he mainly misses fire: I think his life misses fire: he might have been something: he comes near to being something: but he never arrives.

John Burroughs

Look at Thoreau. Even his love of nature seems of the intellectual order—the bookish, library, fireside—rather than smacking of out of doors. This is not the general view: it is my view. With Burroughs it is different: Burroughs has told me of his youth, spent in one of the still more or less crude counties of New York State, among trees, the corn, the wild flowers. Outdoors taught Burroughs gentle things about men—it had no such effect on Thoreau. After all I suppose outdoors had nothing to do with that difference. The contrast just shows what sort of men Thoreau and Burroughs were to start with. I only mean to say that while I have no distrust of Thoreau I often find myself catching a literary scent off his phrases.

———

John's place by nature would seem to have been from the first out of doors: his best books are the early ones—*Wake-*

Robin, others. But John was never satisfied to remain out of doors—to view field-life—report it. He always had a hankering after problems, explanations, metaphysicalisms— to me an obvious weakening. I never disguised from him or from anybody that I thought it a bad investment. It is true he did this work itself remarkably well—contributed inestimable discoveries, all that—said novel and inviting things: but to me none of it, whatever value it had, had the best value of the man.

———

John has that great quality shared now by the greatest men—the faculty that is the mark of their greatness—not to be too damned sure about anything.

George Eliot

They speak of George Eliot as a "meliorist." That would be no sort of a word to express my attitude towards the universe: that word contains an apology—an apology: and an apology is an impertinence. George Eliot is a great, gentle soul, lacking sunlight.

Leo Tolstoy

Perhaps the strongest point with Tolstoy—this point that most fastens itself upon men, upon me—is this: that here is a man with a conviction—a conviction—on which he planted himself, stakes all, invites assault, affection, hope. That would be a good deal if there was nothing more—

not a hint more: whereas that there *is* more to Tolstoy I
think no one can doubt.

———

There's an ascetic side to Tolstoy which I care very little
for: I honor it—I know what it comes from: but I find
myself getting to my end by another philosophy: in some
ways Tolstoy has cut the cord which unites him with us:
has gone back to medievalism—to the saturninity of the
monkish rites: not a return to nature—no: a return to the
sty. But Tolstoy is a world force—an immense vehement
first energy driving to the fulfillment of a great purpose.

———

I confess the book [*The Kreuzer Sonata*] has taken a strong
hold of me—it has opened my eyes, made me feel that we
have a master with us—a master as great as any. I know
of no one who writes in English as he writes, or has ever
so written: with such power, such nature, such absence of
calculations. I feel that it is a picture of high life—a touch
at the heart of so-called society—true in vein, in throb,
in all colors and scenes. I am quite disposed to endorse
it, too, for often it has come to me, the brutishness of the
Orientalism, that gives man any monopoly he chooses
with woman—that excites in him such a passion, frenzy,
of monopoly, as breaks and wrecks her best sympathies
and hopes. As to the indecency, I am astonished that even
the blatherskites who attempted to suppress it should see it

in that light: it is incredible, it is stupid, foolish to the last degree. If the book is as I read it in a translation where something certainly is lost, what must it not be in its original tongue?

Russian literature

A literature in some respects the greatest—but all of it, as the Frenchman says—yes, all of it, all of it—soaked in pessimism. Not the notion, perhaps, that the world is all going to the bad, absolutely, but that things are in a bad way, need repairing. The Russian is a marvelous character—I watch it very closely, wonderingly—regard it as bread in the making—dough not yet in its final shape—the dish, however, proceeding!

Émile Zola

Zola is only treating of life as a physician treats disease. To the general it's nothing but a question of guts, stains, blood, wounds, horror, pain, nastiness, smut: but not so to the chemist, the surgeon, the doctor—not so—not so. Rather something far higher, finer. The time will come—is already here for some—when all these things will be treated so—will enter in that way upon our conversation—even in parlors—among the sexes. Not to be lugged in, or made nasty, but so dealt with when necessity introduces. Then, perhaps, we will see that Zola is justified—that he was advanced, not retrograde.

Oscar Wilde

I never completely make Wilde out—out for good or bad. He writes exquisitely—is as lucid as a star on a clear night—but there seems to be a little substance lacking at the root—something—what is it? I have no sympathy with the crowd of the scorners who want to crowd him off the earth.

———

I think Oscar Wilde hit upon a splendid thought, or expressed it, while in America: that no first-class fellow wishes to be flattered, aureoled, set upon a throne—but craves to be understood, to be appreciated for his immediate active present power.

———

Everybody's been so in the habit of looking at Wilde cross-eyed, sort of, that they have charged the defect of their vision up against Wilde as a weakness in his character.

Reading

*To put a book in your pocket and off to the seashore
or the forest—that is an ideal pleasure.*

I know I did my best reading when I was alone that way—
off in the woods or on the shore. Long ago, when I was a
young man, Coney Island was a favorite spot. At that time
Coney Island had not the reputation it has now—it was
then a desert island—nobody went there. Oh yes! when I
read, it was in solitude, never in frequented places—except
perhaps, Broadway, on the stage-coaches, where a little
more noise more or less made no difference.

I have long teased my brain with visions of a handsome
little book at last—like the Epictetus—a dear, strong, aro-
matic volume, like the Encheiridion, as it is called, for the
pocket. That would tend to induce people to take me along
with them and read me in the open air: I am nearly always
successful with the reader in the open air.

The best reading seems to need the best open air. When
I was down on the Creek—Timber Creek—and roamed

out and along the water, I always took a book, a little book, however rarely I made use of it. It might have been once, twice: three, four, five, even nine, times: I passed along the same trail and never opened the book: but then there was a tenth time, always, when nothing but a book would do—not tree, or water, or anything else—only a book: and it was for that tenth trip that I carried the book.

———

I used to thrust papers, things, into my pockets: always had a lot of reading matter about my person somewhere: on ferries, cars, anywhere, I would read, read, read: it's a good habit to get into: have you ever noticed how most people absolutely waste most all their spare time?

Leaves of Grass

*I do not think even intelligent people know how much
goes to the making of a book: worry, fret, anxiety—
downright hard work—poverty—finally, nothingness!
It is a story yet to be told.*

Leaves of Grass is a seashore, a mountain, floating cloud,
sweeping river, storm, lightning, passion, freedom—and
all the tremendous, vital, throbbing, resistless, overwhelming, stupendous forces (I hope) included in, implied by,
these.

———

I have no axe to grind—no philosophy to offer—no theory
to expound, in *Leaves of Grass*: all I have written there is
written with reference to America—to the larger America—to an America so inclusive, so sufficient, no phase of
life, no nationality—can escape it. As you know, *Leaves
of Grass* is made up of six or seven stages of life, three
of which—the first three—have had that inestimable
benefit which comes of being fought against, bespattered,
denounced. I have not worked according to any elaborate
plan: have tried rather to fill in the gaps—wherever a gap
was left—wherever a gap appeared—I started out to put

something in it. In what is called poetry—singing—the fellows who go on singing the same old songs, again and again and again—but of the most ancient, worn, poetic stock—get mad as the devil at any suggestion of changed modes.

———

Leaves of Grass is *evolution*—evolution in its most varied, freest, largest sense.

———

As to *Leaves of Grass* I can say—with all its spirit and naturalness, and as the thing blows—the wind blows—that is not the whole story. Spontaneity—spontaneity: that's the word, yet even that word needing to be used after a new sense. I am quite clear that I have broken a way—that I have indicated a path—a new, superiorly new, travel-road heretofore not trod by man. Some one of the German philosophers had said, life is not an achieved fact, but a *becoming*. And *Leaves of Grass* is much like life in that respect. And indeed, old earth herself is still *becoming* and always will be the same. The old poets had spontaneity, too, but it was a spontaneity not of the sort we are after. *Leaves of Grass* attempts the unattempted. Other poets have written and written with unmistakable power, grandeur, but my mark has been a distinct one—must be so recognized. I have no doubt but I have done what I say I have done, whatever else is uncertain and insecure.

———

Leaves of Grass is not spontaneous only—it aims to be, or ought to be, spontaneity itself. Other poets before me have been spontaneous—others nobly spontaneous, simple. But I think the *Leaves* have all that spontaneity—then something deeper still. I don't know that I can set this out in a way to have it understood—indeed, I suspect it is not to be so set out. Must be comprehended, if at all, intuitively—must be felt, visioned. Anyway, made palpable, self-evident, without word or process of logic.

———

You can detach poems from the book and wonder why they were written. But if you see them in their place in the book you know why I wrote them.

———

Leaves of Grass does not lend itself to piecemeal quotation: can only find its reflection in ensemble, ensemble: cannot be rendered by any selection of pretty lines, strange allusions, passages from here and there: it belongs to bulk, mass, unity: must be seen with reference to its eligibility to express world-meanings rather than literary prettiness.

———

Emerson's objections to the outcast passages in *Leaves of Grass* were neither moral nor literary, but were given with an eye to my worldly success. He believed the book would sell—said that the American people should know the book: yes, would know it but for its sex handicap: and he thought he saw the way by which to accomplish what he called "the desirable end." He did not say I should drop a single line—he did not put it that way at all: he asked whether I could consent to eliminate certain popularly objectionable poems and passages. Emerson's position has been misunderstood: he offered absolutely no spiritual argument against the book exactly as it stood. Give it a chance to be seen, give the people a chance to want to see it—that was the gist of his contention. If there was any weakness in his position it was in his idea that the particular poems could be dropped and the *Leaves* remain the *Leaves* still: he did not see the significance of the sex element as I had put it into the book and resolutely there stuck to it—he did not see that if I had cut sex out I might just as well have cut everything out—the full scheme would no longer exist—it would have been violated in its most sensitive spot.

———

I had a funny experience with a publisher in my early days—with the first edition. A fellow there was willing to print it but for a couple of lines which he construed into a disrespectful reference to God Almighty. It has always seemed to me *very* funny because I have never heard a word of complaint against them: nobody has picked them out though they have picked out nearly everything else.

People often speak of the *Leaves* as wanting in religion, but that is not my view of the book—and I ought to know. I think the *Leaves* the most religious book among books: crammed full of faith. What would the *Leaves* be without faith? An empty vessel: faith is its very substance, balance—its one article of assent—its one item of assurance.

Leaves of Grass has had this advantage: it has had a stormy early life. Nothing could make up for the loss of this—it was a priceless privilege. Ease, comfort, acceptation, would have ruined us. Even now the storm is not all down—perhaps better *not* down. However, we will not let the new kindness spoil us: there's yet to see! there's yet to see!

I was once driven down a steep hill by a friend of mine: he hurried the horses along at a breakneck pace, I protesting. "Ain't you afraid to go so fast?" I asked. "No—not a bit of it," he answered: "I'm afraid to go slow. That's the only way I can overcome the difficulties of the road." So it is with the *Leaves*—it must drive on, drive on, without protest, without explanations, without hesitations, on and on—no apologies, no dickers, no compromises—just drive on and on, no matter how rough, how dangerous, the road may be.

———

Leaves of Grass is an iconoclasm, it starts out to shatter the idols of porcelain worshipped by the average poets of our age—not ruthlessly—not wantonly—but to do it seriously, as having a great purpose imposed. I love to go along through the land, taking in all natural objects, events,—noting them. For instance, watching the cow crunching the grass—I can hear its melodious crunch—crunch—its bovine music: the lips, soul, of song as much there as anywhere. And the mother at home knitting her children's stockings: not forgetting the yarn—not omitting the needle. The poet would not have that—it would lack in sound, elegance, what he calls poetic evidence. But for me it is my necessity—it is all music—the *clef* of things—to discriminate—not so much to produce an effect, or that at all—but to state the case—the case of the universe: to seize upon its typical phasings.

———

Leaves of Grass never started out to do anything—has no purpose—has no definite beginning, middle, end. It is reflection, it is statement, it is to see and tell, it is to keep clear of judgments, lessons, school-ways—to be a world, with all the mystery of that, all its movement, all its life. From this standpoint I, myself, often stand in astonishment before the book—am defeated by it—lost in its curious revolutions, its whimsies, its overpowering momentum—

lost as if a stranger, even as I am a stranger on this earth—
driving about with it, knowing nothing of why or result.

———

Leaves of Grass has its own eligibilities—has no narrow
tendencies—at least, that I hope it has not.

———

If I have any doubts at all about *Leaves of Grass* it is in the
matter of the expression of my sympathy for the under-
dog—the vicious, the criminal, the malignant (if there are
any malignant): whether I have made my affirmative feeling about them emphatic enough.

———

The workingman is the average man: if *Leaves of Grass* is
not for the average man it is for nobody: not the average
bad man or average good man: no: the average bad good
man: if I have failed to make that clear then I've missed
my mission for certain.

———

Many even of my friends won't call *Leaves of Grass* poems:
they like me, it—think I am, it is, something, some even
say something considerable, but they won't admit it is
poetry.

———

My *Leaves* mean, that in the end reason, the individual, should have control—hold the reins—not necessarily to use them—but to possess the power: reason, the individual—through these solidarity (the whole race, all times, all lands)—this is the main purport, the spinal creative fact, by which we stand or fall.

———

Howells, James and some others appear to think I rest my philosophy, my democracy, upon braggadocio, noise, rough assertion, such integers. While I would not be afraid to assent to this as a part of the truth I still insist that I am on the whole to be thought of in other terms. I recognize, have always recognized, the importance of the lusty, strong-limbed, big-bodied American of the *Leaves*: I do not abate one atom of that belief now, today. But I hold to something more than that, too, and claim a full, not a partial, judgment upon my work—I am not to be known as a piece of something but as a totality.

———

There is no delicatesse, no aestheticism, about the *Leaves*: they are bits out of life, words, hints, coarse, direct, unmistakable. They must be, can only be, understood as the states must be, can only be, understood—with the traces of their material origin clinging everywhere on them. They emerge out of, with, the material—tally all the great shows of our civilization—stand for them—yet for these, not only as they exist, in pride of material splendor—but in their heroic entanglements. The heroic animality of the *Leaves*—it is before all necessary to grapple with, absorb, that quality—for it comes before all the rest.

———

Leaves of Grass may be only an indication—a forerunner—a crude offender against the usual canons—a barbaric road-breaker—but it still has a place, a season, I am convinced. What is that place? that season? I don't know—I give up guessing.

———

Leaves of Grass is essentially a woman's book: the women do not know it, but every now and then a woman shows that she knows it: it speaks out the necessities, its cry is the cry of the right and wrong of the woman sex—of the woman first of all, of the facts of creation first of all—of the feminine: speaks out loud: warns, encourages, persuades, points the way.

———

There are two things in *Leaves of Grass* which dominate everything else—which give it meaning and coherency—two things, found, I hope, in every page—I was going to say, every word. The first is atmosphere: that what we call phenomena, facts, reason, intellect, are not the explications of life—that that lies deeper, is a more penetrating factor—is deep, deep, deep below all casual eyesight or insight either. The other principle, to call it that, is that man is in process of being—that his justification is not in himself, today, but in something yet to come—something ahead.

Leaves of Grass is not intellectual alone (I do not despise the intellectual—far from it: it is not to be despised—has its uses) nor sympathetic alone (though sympathetic enough, too) nor yet vaguely emotional—least of all this. I have always stood in *Leaves of Grass* for something higher than qualities, particulars. It is atmosphere, unity: it is never to be set down in traits but as a symphony: is no more to be stated by superficial criticism than life itself is to be so stated: is not to be caught by a smart definition or all given up to any one extreme statement.

I am often amazed to discover, when I read *Leaves of Grass*, that it is written not only with reference to our own time but to time to come—new, far-off ages—made ripe and applicable, in fact to meet any age, any time, any land. And that is the heart of the story—the vital steady throb, if it have any touch and reason at all.

Life anyhow, particularly life as we live it these modern days—is a going rapidly from one thing to another—incidents, people: a great *mélange*: there is no doubt *Leaves of Grass* partakes of the character of the time: but whatever the change of position, the man is the same—nothing more is signified for it than transfer, entrance upon other outward contingencics.

My Poetry

I should say, my work, I, stand for, solidarity—*not only
of what are called the White or European peoples, but of
the whole earth—and other earths if there can.*

That is one of my purposes: to show the universal beat of
the poetic. There was the locomotive: how often I heard
of its artificiality—that nothing but dust and iron could
be made of it. I accepted the sneers as a challenge—then
the "Locomotive in Winter." How clearly I remember my
anxiety—to get terms straight, to express the technicality
of the trade, then to infuse all with life. It was a challenge—yes, a challenge—perhaps I was reckless to take
it up. But *something* came of it—whether the thing I was
after or something *less* I do not know.

———

I am very deliberate—I take a good deal of trouble with
words: yes, a good deal: but what I am after is the content
not the music of words. Perhaps the music happens—it
does no harm: I do not go in search of it. Two centuries
back or so much of the poetry passed from lip to lip—was
oral: was literally made to be sung: then the lilt, the formal rhythm, may have been necessary. The case is now

somewhat changed: now, when the poetic work in literature is more than nineteen-twentieths of it by print, the simply tonal aids are not so necessary, or, if necessary, have considerably shifted their character.

———

I'm honest when I say, damn "My Captain" and all the "My Captains" in my book! This is not the first time I have been irritated into saying I'm almost sorry I ever wrote the poem. It has reasons for being—it is a ballad—it sings, sings, in a certain strain with a certain motive—but as for being the best, the very best—God help me! what can the worst be like? A whole volume of "My Captains" instead of a scrap-basket! Well, that's funny, very funny: it don't leave me much room for escape. *I* say that if I'd written a whole volume of "My Captains" I'd deserve to be spanked and sent to bed with the world's compliments—which would be generous treatment, considering what a lame duck book such a book would have been!

———

I have never given any study merely to expression: it has never appealed to me as a thing valuable or significant in itself: I have been deliberate, careful, even laborious: but I have never looked for finish—never fooled with technique more than enough to provide for simply getting through: after that I would not give a twist of my chair for all the rest.

A word is a poem of poems!

I suppose no one but the habitué could grasp fully—
even measurably—the pictorial significance of the piece
["Crossing Brooklyn Ferry"]: no one who has not been
there as I have been, a frequenter of ferry ways, boats,
wharves, men, bustling commerces. I have been there in
the presence of all its thousand and one changes of color:
mine was no casual contact, but the contact of years, love,
association—of childhood, boyhood, manhood, matu-
rity—the sailing on the waters, the going out with the
pilots in their pilot boats, the tripping it to the sea and
back again—Sandy Hook, down to Navesink. Only by
such-gathered lights and shades can anyone really know,
appreciate, enter into, the fine tones of meaning: that is, by
actually living, breathing, bathing, in the life of it!

I do not put "Sands at Seventy" forward to be judged by
the standard of the earlier work in *Leaves of Grass*: the
slide has shifted, the point of view changed: years have
sped. I needed something to taper off with: this seemed to
me the best available: yet I know how differently people
feel about it.

Some of my simplest pieces have created the most noise. I have been told that "A Child Went Forth" was a favorite with Longfellow, but to me there is very little in that poem. That is one of my penalties—to have the real vital utterances, if there are any in me, go undetected.

———

I have my own peculiar affection for *November Boughs*. It is the depository of many dreams and thoughts precious to me—of many sacred aspirational experiences, too holy to be argued about—of sayings, almost of *mots*: of so many unspeakable records, reminiscences, worked into the soil of my matured life and now at last projected in this compact shape. To have such a book—such a book produced in every way according to a feller's simple and unimpeded humors—that has been my idea, is still my idea.

———

The general comment on the book [*November Boughs*] is of the pity-the-old-man order. It is good discipline for a man in the face of such an abuse of criticism to sit down and keep cool. I would rather be damned than be saved by pity.

Literature

*We have plenty of books in America—but about
the literature?—oh! I have my doubts!*

What we want above all—what we finally must and will
insist upon—in future—actual men and women—living,
breathing, hoping, aspiring books—books that so grow
out of personality, magnificence of undivided endowment,
as themselves to become such persons, stand justly in their
names.

What would we do without the sinners? Take them out of
literature and it would be barren.

The *grand* does not appeal to me: I dislike the simply *art*
effect—art for art's sake, like literature for literature's sake,
I object to, not, of course, on prude grounds, but because
literature created on such a principle (and art as well)
removes us from humanity, while only from humanity in
mass can the light come.

I do not value literature as a profession. I feel about literature what Grant did about war. He hated war. I hate literature. I am not a literary West Pointer: I do not love a literary man as a literary man, as a minister of a pulpit loves other ministers because they are ministers: it is a means to an end, that is all there is to it: I never attribute any other significance to it. Even Goethe and Schiller, exalted men, both, very, very, were a little touched by the professional consciousness.

———

The American literary fellow—the American himself—is too smart, cute, sensible, to be totally entrapped. Someday he will shake the whole burden off. But as things are now, none of them possess or even respect the simple, elemental, first-hand, Homeric qualities which lie secure at the base of all real work—of all genuine expression. Of course I do not undervalue the canny qualities, either: the disposition to keep some background in goods, money: it has its place—but no first place—no superior place.

———

I care less and less for books as books—more and more for people as people.

———

To the literary craft—to the men who look upon literature as a thing in itself—clear-cut writing—phrasing—

mastery of expression an end—Hawthorne would have to be an eminent figure—among the best, consummate. But these are to some of us things of the past. We have had men in our century who have taken the wind out of all theories of literature that confine it, restrict it, belittle it: for literature in its deepest sense defies measurement, rules, standards. Victor Hugo was one of these men— daring with the daring. Oh! who could say, doing how much good!

A modern "poem" is as if a proper and fashionable suit of clothes, well made, good cloth, fair linen, a gold watch, etc., were to walk about, demanding audience. The clothes are all well enough; but the objection would be, there is no man in them—no virility there.

Quoting is a thing that gets to be a disease.

The trouble is that writers are too literary—too damned literary. There has grown up—Swinburne I think an apostle of it—the doctrine (you have heard of it? it is dinned everywhere), art for art's sake: think of it—art for art's sake. Let a man really accept that—let that really be his ruling thought—and he is lost.

———

Politics for politics' sake, church for church's sake, talk for talk's sake, government for government's sake: state it any way you choose it becomes offensive: it's all out of the same pit. Instead of regarding literature as only a weapon, an instrument, in the service of something larger than itself, it looks upon itself as an end—as a fact to be finally worshipped, adored. To me that's all a horrible blasphemy—a bad-smelling apostasy.

———

It is as if we should fix our eyes on one of the stars there: should say: Let that be the only star: let that stand alone in glory, purpose, sacredness: let all the rest be wiped out: let that alone be declared legitimate: let that alone be our guide. Yet there are millions of other stars in the heavens: millions: some as great, some greater: perhaps some we do not see surpassing the best we see: so there are writers—countless writers: some swept away, lost forever: some neglected: some yet to be recognized for what they are.

———

Literature is big only in one way—when used as an aid in the growth of the humanities—a furthering of the cause of the masses—a means whereby men may be revealed to each other as brothers.

Critics

We must get used to the howlers—there's enough to do,
not to busy with their demonstrations. Settle your case
with yourself —then go ahead—the howl,
the rest, what-not, won't hurt.

I am always concerned over any interference with the expression of opinion: I want the utmost freedom —even the utmost license—rather than any censorship: censorship is always ignorant, always bad: whether the censor is a man of virtue or a hypocrite seems to make no difference: the evil is always evil. Under any responsible social order decency will always take care of itself. I've suffered enough myself from the censors to know the facts at first hand.

—

I hate all censorships, big and little: I'd rather have everything rotten than everything hypocritical or puritanical, if that was the alternative, as it is not. I'd dismiss all monitors, guardians, without any ceremony whatsoever.

—

When I think of the critics I never fail to be reminded of Heine's canon of criticism. Oh! it is superb—splendid.

Heine would ask: What did this certain man stand for, set out to do? And then would ask further: Did he do that—do it honestly, his own way, with success? The code of the newspaper critic has nothing of Heine in it. Every whipper-snapper of a reviewer, instead of trying to get at the motive of a book or an incident, sets out sharply to abuse a fellow because he don't accomplish what he never aimed for and sometimes would not have if he could.

———

I suppose every writer has more or less the same experience: the world says jump and he must jump—the world says die and he is dead.

Art and Artists

What is art? Is it one thing or all things?

You would think that if an artist wished to make a picture of me—of anyone—he would seize upon me just as I am—skin, bones, hair, coat, pants, all—but no—somehow that does not satisfy them—nature can be improved upon—and so they improve and improve and improve, till all the nature is improved out of a picture.

———◆———

I think, all—the Italian laborer on the street, the woman with her child, the curbstones out here—all is for art.

———◆———

To some things in art—Holy Families, Roman chariot races, lords, ladies, all that—I stand a witness against. *We* ought attest our opposition to them, unalterably—not opposition to their past, which was legitimate enough, but to their importance for the present. Of course they have had their place—their world—but that time is gone—all gone. The saddest part about it is, that they still have a following, a constituency.

———

The devil with all the artists—or most all—is that they lack veracity—seem to feel under no obligation to produce things as they see them but rather to color up and up, till the public eye is properly titivated. How can there be true art on this basis?—first-class art by first-class men?

———

Art now is all made with reference to social conventions— the notions, instincts, of parlors, gentlemen, ladies. It does not come direct from nature, but through *media*: receptions, carpets, elegant, showy outsideness. And [Frans] Hals, none of these old fellows (broad as breadth) could have worked, done, what they did, from such inspiration, background.

———

[Jean-François] Millet is my painter: he belongs to me: I have written Walt Whitman all over him. How about that? or is it the other way about? Has he written Millet all over me?

———

Millet—he's a whole religion in himself: the best of democracy, the best of all well-bottomed faith, is in his pictures. The man who knows his Millet needs no creed. . . . The *Leaves* are really only Millet in another form—they are the Millet that Walt Whitman has succeeded in putting into words.

———————

Millet's color sense was opulent, thorough, uncompromising, yet not gaudy—never gilt and glitter: emphatic only as nature is emphatic. I felt the masterfulness of *The Sowers*: its dark grays: not overwrought anywhere: true always to its own truth—borrowing nothing: impressive in its unique majesty of expression. I said to myself then, I say it over to myself now, that I can at last understand the French Revolution—now realize the great powers that lay back of it, explain it—its great far-stretching past. I said to myself then, I can realize now, that there can be no depth of feeling, sympathy, emotional appeal, present in a picture, a painting, anywhere, anytime, going beyond these: here is the fact incarnate.

———————

There is one of Millet's pictures— not so well known—I have seen it—which seems to me the gem of his creations—at least, of such as I have known. The plot of it was simply this—a girl going home with the cows of an evening—a small stream running lazily along—the cattle tempted forward to the water, mildly drinking. I can conceive of nothing more directly encountered in nature than this piece—its simplicity, its grand treatment, the atmosphere, the time of day: not a break in the power of its statement. I looked at it long and long—was fascinated—fascinated to it—could hardly leave it at all. This picture more than any other to my judgment confirmed Millet—justified his position, heroism—assured his future.

———

The minute [Junius] Booth would step on the stage, you would forget his physical proportions. He was much smaller than Edwin. It was singular of him, too, that though so little—though so often on the stage with a crowd of people—he was never lost in the crowd. The actors used to ask him where they should stand and he would say—use your own judgment about that—stand anywhere, so you are not in my way—I will reach you.

———

I never knew of but one artist, and that's Tom Eakins, who could resist the temptation to see what they think ought to be rather than what is.

———

Eakins! How nobly he conforms to the Carlylean standards!—the standards which declare: you will come to this first in doubt, chagrin, perhaps: but here is an art that is nature—that will grow, grow, grow upon you: develop as you develop—is finally all opened to you as a flower!

Who can look at Eakins at the start and be satisfied?—but looking longer, revelation comes—little by little discovery, discovery.

Eakins is not a painter, he is a force.

The photograph has this advantage: it lets nature have its way: the botheration with the painters is that they don't want to let nature have its way: they want to make nature let them have their way.

Nothing can be predicated of a photo—it hits if it hits, not otherwise. It seems true of all photos, that you can't start out to produce any certain effect: you must submit to circumstances!

Self-Reliance

I go my own way—not because I think it the only way,
or even the right way, but because it is my way.

I am always in favor of having a fellow do what he is
strongly bent on doing—what comes to him as a duty;
what he feels he must do, that by all odds he is bound to
do—bound. That has been my course from the first—to
write what I must write—not hesitatingly but decisively—
and will be, I'm sure.

———

The objections to me are the objections made to all men
who choose to go their own road—make their own choice
of methods.

———

When once I am convinced I never let go: I had to pay
much for what I got but what I got made what I paid for it
much as it was seem cheap. I had to give up health for it—
my body—the vitality of my physical self: oh! much had
to go—much that was inestimable, that no man should
give up until there is no longer any help for it: had to give
that up: all that: and what did I get for it? I never weighed

what I gave for what I got but I am satisfied with what I got.

———

I wouldn't know what to do, how to comport myself, if I lived long enough to become accepted, to get in demand, to ride the crest of the wave. I would have to go scratching, questioning, hitching about, to see if this was the real critter, the old Walt Whitman—to see if Walt Whitman had not suffered a destructive transformation—become apostate, formal, reconciled to the conventions, subdued from the old independence. I have adjusted myself to the negative condition—have adjusted myself for opposition, denunciation, suspicion: the revolution, therefore, would have to be very violent indeed to whip me round to the other situation.

———

I always have said—that I care nothing for the public, yet in a sense care for it a good deal. The public has little to do with my acts, deeds, words. I long ago saw that if I was to do anything at all I must disregard the howling throng—must go my own road, flinging back no bitter retort, but declaring myself unalterably whatever happened.

———

I like advice, comment, criticism from all sides: like to hear what is being said, for I see that everything that is said has reason with it—the reason at least to be heard. But after hearing all that is told me, then I like to demonstrate that I hold the reins, that I know the journey's end and drive accordingly. There's that resistance in me under the simplest circumstance. It perhaps has a value, too.

———

People get accustomed to a certain order of traditions, forms: they think these a part of nature, or nature itself— that they are never to be displaced, are eternal: they will not be easily shaken out of their conviction even when they know all their vitality has departed.

———

Here, today, at the end, with the book closed or closing, I glory in the surrender—have no regrets, have nothing to recall.

Egotism

*A man has sometimes to whistle very loud
to keep a stiff upper lip.*

One's egotism carries him a great way towards endurance. It is so with me—I have stuck and stuck—through a something within me which my enemies would think hopeless conceit.

———

A thing Sarrazin takes up boldly is the *egotism*: and as I grow older, I dare more in that respect myself—am less afraid of accusation—am less afraid to be egotist—to let the horses go, so to speak. It arises out of more positive if not new convictions. I know no one who has so heroically accepted that phase.

———

A certain amount of egotism is necessary—but for having it, we never could have endured the strain—passed unharmed through the fire—especially in the years when *Leaves of Grass* stood alone, unfriended but by me.

———

I hate anything like bombast: I hate too much flag flying, hurrahing—such things: I have been accused of blowing my own horn: maybe I'm guilty—just a little bit: I don't stand too hard and fast for behavior: yet I go slow when it comes to the pinch: I don't want to practice self-exaltation. William [O'Connor] used to say: "Walt, you're entitled to it: nobody will do it for you: do it for yourself."

Startle, strikingness, brilliancy, are not factors in my appearance—not a touch of them. As for me I think the greatest aid is in my *insouciance*—my utter indifference: my going as if it meant nothing unusual—happening in.

Time was when I had to say big things about myself in order to be honest with the world—in order to keep in a good frame of mind until the world caught up.

Self-Reflection

No one could have more doubts of me than I have of myself:
I'm not sure of anything except my intentions.

Sometimes I forget myself, you see—go on like any other scarifying quarreller: berate people for not doing what they are not prepared to do: expecting them to reach way beyond themselves. I know it's not reasonable: will not hurry the world along beyond its pace. Then there remains the other reflection: maybe I'm not so far ahead as I think I am—maybe Walt Whitman's not ahead of the world at all—maybe the world's ahead of Walt Whitman: maybe it's with the world, not with Walt Whitman, to complain: who knows?

———

It does a man good to turn himself inside out once in a while: to sort of turn the tables on himself: to look at himself through other eyes—especially skeptical eyes, if he can. It takes a good deal of resolution to do it: yet it should be done—no one is safe until he can give himself such a drubbing: until he can shock himself out of his complacency. Think how we go on believing in ourselves—which in the main is all right (what could we ever do if we didn't believe in ourselves?): but if we don't look out we develop a bumptious bigotry—a colossal self-satisfaction, which is worse for a man than being a damned scoundrel.

———

The great function of the critic is to say bright things— sparkle, effervesce: probably three-quarters, perhaps even more, of them do not take the trouble to examine what they start out to criticize—to judge a man from his own standpoint, to even find out what that standpoint is. I sometimes ask myself: "Am I not too one of the worst of those offenders? have not I too said this, that, where silence would have been better, honester?"

———

I have never praised myself where I would not if I had been somebody else: I have merely looked myself over and repeated candidly what I saw—the mean things and the good things: I did so in the *Leaves*, I have done so in other places: candidly faced the life in myself—my own possibilities, probabilities: reckoned up my own account, so to speak. I know this is unusual: but is it wrong? Why should not everybody do it?

———

I never get nervous: I have heard about it in others: it never affects me. I remember, my friends always remarked it, that in crises, I never was disturbed or gave out any consciousness of danger—as, indeed, I did not feel it. It has always been so: it is a part of my ancestral quality persisting and saving. Yet, Horace, this does not mean—must not be supposed to prove—that I am not susceptible—on the contrary, I am very susceptible—few more so: alive to all acts, persons, influences.

———

I am not a saint—have never been guilty of setting up for a saint. I find some of my friends—some of the ardent eulogists—making very many claims for me which I would not make for myself. Neither do I feel that I am such an awful sinner: I have made mistakes—many of them: led an average human life: not too good, not too bad—just a so-so sort of life. I don't spend much time wondering whether I should not have been better or might not have been worse.

———

No one knows what is hidden away in me as I do: I tell you all this man says is true, every word of it—and more, too, if he had chosen to go farther. You must not suppose that because I suppress the evidences of it that it does not exist—that there are not in me, too, as much as in anyone, wild growths of poison flowers, mad passions of villainy, to be fought and thrown in the defence of virtue.

———

My disposition is to hear all—the worst word that is said—the ignorantest—whatever. That there's nothing, in fact, I should so regret as not to know how affairs are regarded. For I know—never hide from myself—how much is to be said on the other side—antagonistically—however cherished our own notions are.

———

They call it my procrastination—it has always been my habit. And while my friends always declare that I have lost much by it—my best opportunities, even—I feel for myself that I have gained, too—that in some large sense it has been the making of me—has been me, in fact.

———

I have always craved to hear the damndest that could be said of me, and the damndest has been said, I do believe. I have welcomed all that could be advanced, as much can well be, I know. Once or twice things have been said with such insight, I have ordered my course accordingly.

———

I am the sort of man who, however stubborn, is yet never oversure of himself: I am still only on the edge of the world—the margin of its margin, so to speak: I haven't solidified myself: a little push and I would be over again: I do not feel that I have achieved what might be called a standing: far from that.

Women

Freedom must be for the women as well as the men.

I look to see woman take her place in literature, in art—show what are her innate potencies, powers, attributes.

What is woman's place, function, in the complexity of our social life? Can women create, as man creates, in the arts? rank with the master craftsmen? . . . It has been a historic question. Well—George Eliot, George Sand, have answered it: have contradicted the denial with a supreme affirmation.

It would seem about time something was done in the direction of the recognition of the women: for some of us to dwell upon the lives of noble big women. History teems with accounts of big men—genius, talent—of the he-critters, but the women go unmentioned. Yet how much they deserve! I know from time to time there are spasms of virtue—some fellow sets up to describe the salons—as in one of the magazines lately but what is that? I have no admiration for the formal elegant lives of salons. I have in

mind the noble plain women I have met—*many* of them—
women to whom the *word* "literature" even is unknown;
mothers of families—mistresses of households—out over
the country—on farms, in the villages: marvellous man-
agers—tender, wise, pure, high—the salt of our civilization. I have often resolved to write this up myself, but am
stayed: that would spoil it all to write it up!—and so have
not done it.

———

Oh! I think the sweetest, sanest, perfectest, whollest,
majestic-est of all characters are the mothers of children.
Neither saints nor warriors—neither—all history, art, literature, has so far been devoted to such. Now comes a new
age, new recognitions—the age of the mothers.

Love

Shall we be less than the sun—shall we pause to inquire all the love out of life?

It's wonderful how true it is that a man can't go anywhere without taking himself along and without finding love meeting him more than half way. It gives you a new intimation of the providences to become the subject of such an ingratiating hospitality: it makes the big world littler—it knits all the fragments together: it makes the little world bigger—it expands the arc of comradery.

———

I loved Emerson for his personality and I always felt that he loved me for something I brought him from the rush of the big cities and the mass of men. We used to walk together, dine together, argue, even, in a sort of a way, though neither one of us was much of an arguer. We were not much for repartee or sallies or what people ordinarily call humor, but we got along together beautifully—the atmosphere was always sweet, I don't mind saying it, both on Emerson's side and mine: we had no friction—there was no kind of fight in us for each other—we were like two Quakers together.

———

A man's family is the people who love him—the people who comprehend him.

———

The letters, my letters, sent to the boys, to others, in the days of the War, stir up memories that are both painful and joyous. That was the sort of work I always did with the most relish: I think there is nothing beyond the comrade—the man, the woman: nothing beyond: even our lovers must be comrades: even our wives, husbands: even our fathers, mothers: we can't stay together, feel satisfied, grow bigger, on any other basis.

———

A woman I knew once asked a man to give her a child: she was greatly in love with him: it was not done: he did not care that much for her: he said to her, "all children should be love children": then he thought she might repent if the thing was done: after his refusal she said: "Now I suppose you despise me." He said: "Despise you? no: I respect you: I feel that you have conferred the highest honor on me." Years after, he met her again. She was married—had children. But she said to him: "I still love my dream-child best."

———

I don't know what about marriage (the state, the church, marriage) but about love—well, love will always take care of itself: it does not need censors, monitors, guardians.

———

The sun shines, shines, shines: it has no question to ask of whore, of murderer, of anyone. It gives what it has, yielding to each after its necessity.

Sex

*Damn the expurgated books! I say damn 'em! The dirtiest
book in all the world is the expurgated book!*

Sex is a red rag to most people. It takes some time to get
accustomed to me, but if the folks will only persevere they
will finally feel right comfortable in my presence. "Children of Adam"—the poems—are very innocent: they will
not shake down a house. A man was here the other day
who asked me: "Don't you feel rather sorry on the whole
that you wrote the sex poems?" I answered him by ask-
ing another question: "Don't you feel rather sorry on the
whole that I am Walt Whitman?"

———

All this fear of indecency, all this noise about purity and
sex and the social order and the Comstockism particular
and general is nasty—too nasty to make any compromise
with. I never come up against it but I think of what [Hein-
rich] Heine said to a woman who had expressed to him
some suspicion about the body. "Madame," said Heine,
"are we not all naked under our clothes?"

———

We have got so in our civilization, so-called (which is no civilization at all) that we are afraid to face the body and its issues—when we shrink from the realities of our bodily life: when we refer the functions of the man and the woman, their sex, their passion, their normal necessary desires, to something which is to be kept in the dark and lied about instead of being avowed and gloried in.

———

The body is stubborn: it craves bodily presences: it has its own peculiar tenacities—we might say aspirations as well as desires.

———

Obscenity? Obscene? Oh! Is the surgeon's knife obscene? It might just as well be said of the one as the other. This is a picture to the life, a cut to the bone. It is not a pleasant book: it is horrible, horrible, in its truth, its graphic power.

———

There was one of the department heads at Washington who conceived a great dislike for the word *virile*—gave out orders that it should not be used in any of the documents issuing from that department. I was very curious about it, and asked him once how his antipathy (and it was a *virile* antipathy!) arose. He said that he hated the word—that it called up in him images of everything filthy, nasty, vile. It was very amusing. I remarked to him: "Did it never occur to you that the fault is in you and not in the word? *I* use the word—like it—am never once brought by it into touch with the images you speak of." But he was obdurate—remarking only: "Well—whatever: I won't have it! I hate the word!" And yet he was a man of force, filled his place well, in all the usual ways was sound and sensible.

I often say to myself about Calamus—perhaps it means more or less than what I thought myself—means different: perhaps I don't know what it all means—perhaps never did know.

Any demonstration between men—any: it is always misjudged: people come to conclusions about it: they know nothing, there is nothing to be known; nothing except what might just as well be known: yet they shake their wise heads—they meet, gossip, generate slander: they know what is not to be known—they see what is not to be seen: so they confide in each other, tell the awful truth: the old women men, the old men women, the guessers, the false-witnesses—the whole caboodle of liars and fools.

"Calamus" is a Latin word—much used in Old English writing, however. I like it much—it is to me, for my intentions, indispensible—the sun revolves about it, it is a timber of the ship—not there alone in that one series of poems, but in all, belonging to all. It is one of the United States—it is the quality which makes the states whole—it is the thin thread—but, oh! the significant thread!—by which the nation is held together, a chain of comrades; it could no more be dispensed with than the ship entire.

———

I have heard nothing but expurgate, expurgate, expurgate, from the day I started. Everybody wants to expurgate something—this, that, the other thing. If I accepted all the suggestions there wouldn't be one leaf of the *Leaves* left— and if I accepted one why shouldn't I accept all? Expurgate, expurgate, expurgate! I've heard that till I'm deaf with it. Who didn't say expurgate? Rossetti said expurgate and I yielded. Rossetti was honest, I was honest—we both made a mistake. It is damnable and vulgar—the mere suggestion is an outrage. Expurgation is apology—yes, surrender—yes, an admission that something or other was wrong. Emerson said expurgate—I said no, no. I have lived to regret my Rossetti yes—I have not lived to regret my Emerson no. Expurgate, expurgate, expurgate—apologize, apologize: get down on your knees.

———

Emerson was quite vigorous in talking about the critics— talking with me: he said: "I seem to mystify them—rather mystify than antagonize them": which I guess was true. I seem to make them mad—rile them: I mystify them, too, but they don't know it: they only know I am vile, indecent, perverted, adulterous.

The world now can have no idea of the bitterness of the feeling against me in those early days. I was a tough—obscene: indeed, it was my obscenity, libidinousness, all that, upon which they made up their charges.

It has always been a puzzle to me why people think that because I wrote "Children of Adam," *Leaves of Grass*, I must perforce be interested in all the literature of rape, all the pornograph of vile minds. I have not only been made a target by those who despised me but a victim of violent interpretation by those who condoned me.

What do you call free love? There's no other kind of love, is there? As to the next step—who knows what it means? I only feel sure of one thing: that we won't go back: that the women will take care of sex things—make them what they choose: man has very little to do with it except to conform.

I think Swedenborg was right when he said there was a close connection—a very close connection—between the state we call religious ecstasy and the desire to copulate. I find Swedenborg confirmed in all my experience. It is a peculiar discovery. It was Burns—Whittier's friend Burns—who said in a couple of lines of one of his poems, I'd rather cause the birth of one than the death of 20! And that would be my doctrine, too!

———

We have gone on for so long hurting the body that the job of rehabilitating it seems prodigious if not impossible. The time will come when the whole affair of sex—copulation, reproduction—will be treated with the respect to which it is entitled. Instead of meaning shame and being apologized for it will mean purity and will be glorified.

———

The woman who has denied the best of herself—the woman who has discredited the animal want, the eager physical hunger, the wish of that which though we will not allow it to be freely spoken of is still the basis of all that makes life worth while and advances the horizon of discovery. Sex: sex: sex: whether you sing or make a machine, or go to the North Pole, or love your mother, or build a house, or black shoes, or anything—anything at all—it's sex, sex, sex: sex is the root of it all: sex—the coming together of men and women: sex: sex.

Friendship

I am the friend of all.

I have no time for despair—not even for the fidgets. If my friends would understand me—if the group of my friends wished to recognize the salient meanings—if they thought it worth while—I should say they must consider how much I carry in me that is peculiar, indigenous, to America—and America cannot afford to despair, to get gloomy, whatever comes to the top.

———

Have you never noticed the tendency in naturalists—men who live out of doors, in the woods, the supposedly forest life: the tendency towards depression, if not actually depression itself? the taint of it? Could it be that a withdrawal from human comradeship had something to do with this?

———

I have had to spend a good deal of time for thirty years thinking of my enemies: they have made me think of them: even when I have tried to forget I had any enemies, have been compelled to reckon with them. But when I turn about and look at my friends—the friends I have had: how sacred, stern, noble, they have been: the few of them: when I have thought of them I have realized the intrinsic immensity of the human spirit and felt as if I lived environed by gods.

———

You often hear me object to gush: I like love, I like freedom, I like any honest emotional utterance—but I hate to have people come at me with malice—throw themselves into my arms—insist upon themselves, upon their affection. I shy at it.

———

Most of my friends have been thinkers—people of the highest, though not of the professional, poetic nature. The great literary leaders—most of them—had no idea that I could be taken seriously and refused to condone my existence. If God Almighty was willing to be responsible for me, well and good: but as for them—they would have no Walt Whitman: their skirts were clean.

———

I never feel unhappy over what is unavoidable: I have no more right to expect things of my family than my family has to expect things of me: we are simply what we are: we do not always run together like two rivers: we are not alike: that's the part and the whole of it. My relations with Nelly and William [O'Connor] were quite exceptional: extended to both phases—the personal, the general: they were my unvarying partisans, my unshakable lovers—my espousers: William, Nelly: William so like a great doing out of the eternal—a withering blast to my enemies, a cooling zephyr to my friends.

———

The older I grow, the broader, deeper, larger that word Solidarity is impressed on my convictions—Solidarity: where can one produce its substitute? To me, the largest word in human resources—the largest word in the catalogue—fullest of meaning, potential, all-inclusive.

Democracy

I have great faith in the masses—beneath all the froth, illiteracy, worse, there is something latent—now and then to break forth—which cannot be defied, which saves us at last.

To me there is something curious, indescribably divine, in the compound individuality that is in every one. I suppose there are four hundred leaves of grass, one after another, contradictory, held together by that iron band—individuality, personality, identity.

———

We can't get on with a world of masters: we want men—a world of men: backbone men—the workers, the doers, the humbles: we want them. The ornamental classes make a lot of noise but they create nothing: you may crack a whip over men and you may be useless nevertheless: lots in business that passes for ability is only brutality: don't forget that—you masters: you are not so damned clever as you think: you're only coarse, cruel, wanton: that's all: that's all.

———

The tragedies of the average man—the tragedies of everyday—the tragedies of war and peace—the obscured, the lost, tragedies: they are all cut out of the same goods. I think too much is made of the execution of Jesus Christ. I know Jesus Christ would not have approved of this himself: he knew that his life was only another life, any other life, told big; he never wished to shine, especially to shine at the general expense.

———————

How people may get to believe they are saying a new thing when they are simply rehashing a very ancient text. Take Democracy, for instance: the American, the average American, thinks he has a new idea. The truth is that even our proud modern definitions of democracy are antiquated—can be heard reflected in the language of the Elizabethan period in England—in the atmosphere created by Bacon, Ben Jonson, and the rest of that crowd. I would not like to say there might not have been latent in the utterances of that group of men the seed stuff of our American liberty—not to speak of the still older suggestions of it to be found in Greek and Roman sources.

———————

Before I was sick, particularly in the year or two previous, I was visited a lot by the better class mechanics—I mean the more serious of the mechanics (the more informed, ambitious, instructed). Frequently they would come in and talk and talk, sometimes like a house afire, of their enthusiasms—socialistic, many of them, perhaps most of them, were—very bright, quick, dead in earnest, able to take care of themselves and more too in an argument. They, their like, the crowd of the grave workingmen of our world—they are the hope, the sole hope, the sufficient hope, of our democracy. Before we despair we have to count them in—after we count them in we won't despair. All will adjust itself. But that image of the typical extra fine Britisher—his brown face, his broad deep chest, his ample limbs, his clear eye, his strong independent chest, his ample limbs, his clear eye, his strong independent mien, his resonant voice—still clings to me. One thing we must remember: we were born in the political sense free—they were not: that creates an altogether different atmosphere—is a fact never to be forgotten. We seem in many ways to have grown careless of our freedom. Some day we will have to stir our croppers and fight to be free again!

———

I want the real things to get said and done whether they please me or please anybody in particular or not: the real things: the people's things. I am always outspoken on this point. When I say I even include kings I wouldn't like to be understood as making a plea for kingcraft: I include Carnegie but I would not make a plea for Homestead: God forbid!—yes, I say damn Homestead! But I can't get myself into a personal boil in the matter: I want the arrogant money powers disciplined, called to time: I think

I shall rejoice in anything the people do to demonstrate their contempt for the conditions under which they are despoiled.

———

I have always had an idea that I should some day move off—be alone: finish my life in isolation: it may not seem just like me to say that, but I've felt so: at the last, after my fires were spent. For the most part I have desired to remain in the midst of the hurlyburly—to be where the crowd is: to make use of its magnetism, to borrow life from its magnetism: my heart is always with the people, in the thick of the struggle.

America

If America is not for freedom I do not see what it is for.

America—her clouds, her rivers, her woods—all her origin, purpose, ideals; let it be reflected in the majesty of each individual. Nature exhales; let man exhale—let our America exhale—to do this is her work.

———

There is more, too—the bottom fact of all—the inherent good nature, integrity, sanity of man—residing below, underneath all venoms, poisons, evil wills. Especially as existing in our democratic land, age—in America.

———

It is with America as it is with nature: I believe our institutions can digest, absorb, all elements, good or bad, godlike or devilish, that come along: it seems impossible for nature to fail to make good in the processes peculiar to her: in the same way it is impossible for America to fail to turn the worst luck into best—curses into blessings.

———

I hold to that for America: she is in the position between to do and not to do—she must be individualistic, yet not individualistic—strange as that may seem—paradoxical as it appears. Oh! she needs to go on with caution—wise forethought—to be strong, decisive—yet calm—circumspect.

It is said reproachfully of America that she is material, but that to me is her glory—the body must precede the soul: the body is the other side of the soul.

America, I said many years ago, has accomplished the greatest results in all things except literature—in all features of modern life except literature, which is the greatest, noblest, divinest, of all: and there she is simply an absorber, an automatic listener, with no eye, ear, arm, heart, her own. If it was necessary—I hope to God it will never be necessary—she would excel all other races, states, in military glory, also, sorry as that is, sorry—O sorry—as it is.

The prairies typify America—our land—these States—democracy—freedom, expanse, vista, magnificence, sweep, hospitality.

One of the first points that takes hold on you as you go west is, that here is lots and lots and lots and lots and still lots beyond lots, of land, on which men may spread out as they choose—land limitless—miles and miles and miles and miles and miles—no end!

———————

I have no doubt myself, but by and by the capital will go west—somewhere along the Mississippi—the Missouri: that is the natural play of tendencies: eventually something like this result is inevitable.

———————

Fifty years or so ago—or forty—there was a scheme to connect all America by noble roads—the west to the east—the north to the south—and some of them were even commenced. There are said to be several great roads—roads that will compare with the Roman, the best so far known in history—out around Pittsburgh. But the scheme came to nothing—for soon we had the cars—the great railroads—and then such a thing as a turnpike became vulgar—no one would hear to it. And yet a great road is a great moral agent. Oh! a great road is not the stone merely, or the what-not, that goes to make it—but something more—far more!

———————

America is long suffering, quiet, not quarrelsome, plain, democratic—no great armies—not easily aroused; but once stirred to the deep—once touched at the heart—she is fearful—she sways the fates themselves—yes, till judgment is hers!

———

We ought to invite the world through an open door—all men—yes, even the criminals—giving to everyone a chance—a new outlook. My God! are men always to go on clawing each other—always to go on taxing, stealing, warring, having a class to exclude and a class excluded—always to go on having favorite races, favorite castes—a few people with money here and there—all the rest without anything everywhere?

———

America must welcome all—Chinese, Irish, German, pauper or not, criminal or not—all, all, without exceptions: become an asylum for all who choose to come. We may have drifted away from this principle temporarily but time will bring us back. The tide may rise and rise again and still again and again after that, but at last there is an ebb—the low water comes at last. Think of it—think of it: how little of the land of the United States is cultivated—how much of it is still utterly untilled. When you go West you sometimes travel whole days at lightning speed across vast spaces where not an acre is plowed, not a tree is touched, not a sign of a house is anywhere detected. America is not for special types, for the caste, but for the great mass of people—the vast, surging, hopeful, army of workers. Dare we deny them a home—close the doors in their face—take possession of all and fence it in and then sit down satisfied with our system—convinced that we have solved our problem? I for my part refuse to connect America with such a failure—such a tragedy, for tragedy it would be.

———

America has its purpose: it must serve that purpose to the end: I look upon the future as certain: our people will in the end read all these lessons right: America will stand opposed to everything which means restriction—stand against all policies of exclusion: accept Irish, Chinese— knowing it must not question the logic of its hospitality.

———

The poor Italian immigrants! The popular fury now seems to be applied to them—and what have they done, indeed? I wonder if our people really believe the Chinese menace our institutions—the industrious, quiet, inoffensive Chinese? Maybe our institutions ain't no good if they're as thin-skinned as that.

———

The exclusion of the Chinese, the tariff, prohibition, all that is of one piece, and I for one not only despise it but always denounce it—lose no occasion. The policy which allows some fellow who wishes to make buttons or some fellow who wishes to make tin to go to Washington and set matters up there so that the foreign fellows with their tin and buttons are barred out is no policy of mine.

———

I look ahead seeing for America a bad day—a dark if not stormy day—in which this policy, this restriction, this attempt to draw a line against free speech, free printing, free assembly, will become a weapon of menace to our future.

———

I think patriotism—our patriotism—has never been better defined than by Paine—he hit it off in several places. For instance, where he says—*the world is my country, to do good is my religion*. That is the whole gospel of politics, life.

———

I am very warmly disposed towards the South: I must admit that my instinct of friendship towards the South is almost more than I like to confess: I have very dear friends there: sacred, precious memories: the people there should be considered, even deferred to, instead of browbeaten:

I feel sore, I feel some pain, almost indignation, when I think that yesterday keeps the old brutal idea of subjugation on top. I would be the last one to confuse moral values—to imagine the South impeccable: I don't condone the South where it has gone wrong: its negro slavery—I don't condone that: far from it, I hate it—I have always said so, South and North: but there is another spirit dormant there which it must be the purpose of our civilization to bring forth: it can't, it must not, be killed. It is true there are a lot of us—like you, me, others—in whom there is developed a new camaraderie, fellowship, love: the farther truer idea of the race family, of international unity, of making one country of all countries: but the trouble is that we do not hold the whip hand.

———

If there's anything that will destroy our American people, our States, it will be fraud—the element of fraud. It is the poison, the danger, of our civilization. In Philadelphia—in Camden—rows of shells—not a genuine house among them. Mr. Smith and his wife come along—see a house— it has a neat, dainty facade—all is fair without. Here then is what we want—and they take it. But a year passes— now they see their bargain. It gapes, yawns, strains—not a joint secure. That is one side of our life—a side that makes American boasts farcical.

———

America is assured, apart from politicians, pro or con—or ministers—or bluster. In the masses no want of virility—sanity—that is America's hope.

———◆———

Base-ball is our game: the American game: I connect it with our national character. Sports take people out of doors, get them filled with oxygen—generate some of the brutal customs (so-called brutal customs) which, after all, tend to habituate people to a necessary physical stoicism. We are some ways a dyspeptic, nervous set: anything which will repair such losses may be regarded as a blessing to the race. We want to go out and howl, swear, run, jump, wrestle, even fight, if only by so doing we may improve the guts of the people: the guts, vile as guts are, divine as guts are!

———◆———

It has been my ambition for America that she should permit, excite, high ideals—enlarged views.

———◆———

I wonder if the American people are not the most enterprising on the globe, in history—any land, any age? They seem to be in readiness at all times for all emergencies: places of peril they transform instantly to safeties: certainly a wonderful peculiar gift, in which, in whatever else falling short, they undoubtedly excel, stand at the head.

The Civil War

*I was in the midst of it all—saw war where war is worst—
not on the battlefields, no—in the hospitals: there war is
worst: there I mixed with it: . . . God damn every war:
God damn 'em! God damn 'em!*

The War deeply engaged me: enlisted all my powers,
thoughts, affection: the doubts, anxieties, dubiosities: the
tos and fros, the ups and downs, the heres and theres:
the sad visions, ever approaching, ever appealing: deeply,
unreservedly, commanded me.

———

I never once have questioned the decision that led me into
the War: whatever the years have brought—whatever sick-
ness, what-not—I have accepted the result as inevitable
and right. This is the very centre, circumference, umbi-
licus, of my whole career. You remember Homer—the
divine horses: "Now, Achilles, we'll take you there, see
you safely back again, but only on condition you will not
do this thing again—act unwisely; will be steady, peace-
ful, quiet—cut up no capers": but you know Achilles said:
"No—let what must, come: I must cut up my capers." So

it was with me: I had to cut up my capers. Why, I would not for all the rest have missed those three or four years.

———

My place in Washington was a peculiar one—my reasons for being there, my doing there what I did do. I do not think I quite had my match. People went there for all sorts of reasons, none of which were my reasons: went to convert, to proselyte, to observe, to do good, to sentimentalize, from a sense of duty, from philanthropic motives: women, preachers, emotionalists, gushing girls: and I honor them all—all: knew them, hundreds of them, well, and in many cases came to love them. But no one—at least no one that I met—went just from my own reasons—from a profound conviction of necessity, affinity—coming into closest relations—relations oh! so close and dear!—with the whole strange welter of life gathered to that mad focus. I could not expect to do more for my own part at this late day than collect a little of the driftwood of that epoch and pass it down to the future.

———

O God! that whole damned war business is about nine hundred and ninety nine parts diarrhea to one part glory: the people who like the wars should be compelled to fight the wars: they are hellish business, wars—all wars: Sherman said, War is hell: so it is: any honest man says so—hates war, fighting, bloodletting.

It was the average soldier, after all—the average soldier, north and south—who was the golden swordblade of our war. I remember one man—a sort of teamster—driver of an ambulance. Off from Washington was what was called a convalescent department: I often rode out to it—whenever possible, rode outside, with the driver. There was one man among those who had known Lincoln in his early days— in the Springfield days—had worked in the principal store at Springfield, as clerk, helper, assistant, laborer, I don't know what. It was from him I learned many of my best things about Lincoln. Already at that time Lincoln was a man of some note—had a good home in Springfield—was married—ran things. He would come down to this store to buy. Oh! many's the little items of description this man imparted, how Lincoln appeared then—appeared in his purchasings, his buying this, his not buying that, why he felt he needed one thing, why not another: items, insignificant details, which the man soon understood were of an intense interest to me. This man, occupying a place as teamster, was very subordinate—I don't know whether very poor, but certainly not getting much out of this work. I said to him one day, "Don't you know that Abe Lincoln is big Injun now—that he could do almost anything for you—put you in almost any convenient position?" He answered at once, "Yes, I do!" Then I urged, "Well—why don't you go to see him then—why don't you call? Don't you think he would remember you?" "Oh yes, he would."

"Well, why don't you call, then?" I shall never forget the man's emphasis in replying—the tone of his voice—his look—it was a poem in itself. "What—me call on him? Add to his burdens?—on a man worried from morning to night not only by his great cares but by applicants for this, applicants for that, applicants for the other thing? No indeed: I could never do it!" It was a flash out of heaven: the man was a hero to me at once.

———

The telegraph corps in the war: no division of the service more intricate—nobler—requiring more courage, penetration, faithfulness: its necessity, too, a very high development of the moral sense—the sense of duty, virtue. These fellows—19, 20, 21—to 26 or 27—boys and men—knew everything, could tell everything or anything—yet, so far as I know, there is no record of betrayal in the whole story of the war—nor this, even at times when the departments in Washington were full of traitors—when knowledge was barter—when every secret seemed sold. But who hears of these men now?—heard of them then? The memory of it, almost, is wiped out.

———

Some of my best friends in the hospitals were probably Southern boys. I remember one in particular, right off—a Kentucky youngster (a mere youngster), illiterate, extremely: I wrote several letters for him to his parents, friends: fine, honest, ardent, chivalrous. I found myself loving him like a son: he used to kiss me good night—kiss me. He got well, he passed out with the crowd, went home, the war was over. We never met again. Oh! I could tell you a hundred such tales. I don't know but I've put this case, this Kentucky boy's case, into *Two Rivulets*: maybe not—there's a lot of that stuff I never put down anywhere—some of the best of it. I could only give the typical cases.

———

There is one thing I shall always regret for myself—always reproach myself for having neglected. I had some brief experience in the South—an intimate experience while it lasted—was convinced that the "poor white" there, so-called, had never had justice done him in our histories, newspapers, official documents—in our war-talk and after war-talk. Everybody everywhere seems to be interested in crushing him down and keeping him crushed down. If I could I would even undertake the job yet—even yet make some record on its side to show how I hate the tyranny that has oppressed it—pay some tribute to a class so thoroughly, so universally, misunderstood. The horrible patois attributed to the "poor white" there in the South (and not to them only—to Western and Northern classes also) I never found—never encountered. I discovered courtesy, chivalry, generosity, and by no means such external ugliness as is usually charged to them. In fact, all my experiences

South—all my experiences in the hospitals, among the soldiers in the crowds of the cities, with the masses, in the great centers of population—allowing for all idiosyncrasies, idiocrasies, passions, what-not, the very worst—have only served to confirm my faith in man—in the average of men. Take the hospital drill I went through—take the mixtures of men there, men often supposed to be of contrary types—how impressive was the fact of their likeness, their uniformity of essential nature—the same basic traits in them all—in the Northern man, in the Southern man, in the Western man—all of one instinct, one color—addicted to the same vices, ennobled by the same virtues: the dignity, courtesy, open-handedness, radical in all, beautiful in all. When I first went to Washington I had a great dislike for the typical Yankee—had always had it, years back from the start—but in my very first contact with the human Yankee all my prejudices were put to flight.

The War was the boil—that was all: not the root. The War was not the cause of the War: the cause lay deeper—could not have been shifted from its purposes. There are cute historical writers—very cute ones, the best of the whole group—who trace events in modern history back to the Crusades—establish a definite and conclusive connection. So it must be with our Rebellion: to try to consider it without considering what preceded it is only to dally with the truth.

───◆───

I have seen the preparations for the great dinners of state at Washington—then the sumptuous fare: the swell military grandees, the political fol-de-rol, the brilliant lights—social form and superficial manners: it is all very staggering in a hollow sort of way. But I have seen something more convincing than that—a simple group of half a dozen veterans gathered about a plain board table, with plenty and good to eat, in a house that was perfectly plain, telling their stories—stories of things done and missed being done, stories of heroism and cowardice, stories of meanness and generosity—stories, yes, of death, of suffering, of sacrifice: all told so quietly, too, with no feathers, no tufts, no one wanting to call special attention to himself—everything being kept on a level lower than false ostentation, higher than false humility.

───◆───

Why—there was Grant—see how he went about his work, defied the rules, played the game his own way—did all the things the best generals told him he should not do—and won out! Suppose the poet is warned, warned, warned, and wins out?

───◆───

Grant was the typical Western man: the plainest, the most efficient: was the least imposed upon by appearances, was most impressive in the severe simplicity of his flannel shirt and his utter disregard for formal military etiquette. Lee had great qualities his own but these were the greatest. I could appreciate such contrasts: I lived in the time, on the spot: I lived in the midst of the life and death vigils of those fearful years—in the camps, in the hospitals, in the fiercest ferment of events.

———

It seems to me Napoleonicism—to make a word—means the very thing praised in Grant. The old fellows would have said—"Cross the Alps? It is impossible—fatuous!" Which only excited Napoleon the more to say, "Impossible? Then we will do it!"—and other impossible things he did—till at last his mastership could not be denied. All genius defies the rules—makes its own passage—is its own precedent.

———

[Jefferson] Davis was absolutely without lubricity. Was like a general, having made a mistake, with time for retrieval—but was too proud to unbend, to acknowledge his mistake. If you grant that, then goodby science—to the devil with progress! The top-most glory of science, our science, today—is its spirit of tolerance—its broad human spirit of acceptance—its admission equally of every view—making dogma of none. Davis was of a damned bad type—of the type which, liking cabbage (to give a homely instance) or onions, would damn anybody who does not. But that is not modern—that is not up to us—we have reached beyond and beyond. The South has had some of the best samples and some of the meanest. I have seen Davis often—we measured him long ago. It would not be well to have an America of such men.

———

Davis was representative: he must bear the onus of that. Besides, Davis is alive: he has perfect freedom: he goes where he wills: every now and then we read accounts of new speeches by him: he is everywhere down South warmly received——applauded to the echo—the echo itself echoed. What more could he have? This has been paralleled nowhere in the world: in any other country on the globe the whole batch of the Confederate leaders would have had their heads cut off.

———

Have you ever seen [William Tecumseh] Sherman? It is necessary to see him in order to realize the Norse make-up of the man—the hauteur—noble, yet democratic: a hauteur I have always hoped I, too, might possess. Try to picture Sherman—seamy, sinewy, in style—a bit of stern open air made up in the image of a man. The best of Sherman was best in the war but has not been destroyed in peace—though peace brought with it military reviews, banquets, bouquets, women, flirtations, flattery. I can see Sherman now, at the head of the line, on Pennsylvania Avenue, the day the army filed before Lincoln—the silent Sherman riding beyond his aides. Yes, Sherman is all very well: I respect him. But, after all, Sheridan was the Napoleonic figure of the war—not subjected to the last tests (though I am sure he would have been equal to them) but adequate, it seemed, to whatever duty arose. That is where I place Sheridan—among Napoleonic things. The real military figure of the war, counting the man in, was Grant, whose homely manners, dislike for military frippery—for every form of ostentation, in war and peace— amounted to genius.

———

[Sherman] was a warrior—Normanesque, I was going to say: he seemed to me like a Norman baron, lord of many acres—with adherents, servitors—all that—something of grandeur, hauteur, haughtiness. That was the man. I think I have told you a story about him—I shall tell it again—it throws the whole character in relief. It was in the review of the troops after the war—in Washington—I can see the day, the long, winding, noble procession—the sky, people, earth. Sherman was at the head of the line—rode, uniformed, a noble animal. Kept a distance of perhaps 15 feet between his own place and the file of aides. These aides spread entirely across Pennsylvania Avenue—all mounted.

In front of Welland's a woman set forth from the crowd—straight up to the General's horse—gave him a bunch of flowers. It all comes back to me—vivid—powerful—the etched features of the scene: he took the flowers, curtsied, put them—an instant only—to his nose—then held them out and back with his hand, so for the instant I did not know what it meant, but before I needed to ask, one of the aides galloped out of the line, up to the General, took the flowers from him, returned to his place again. What could better present the man than that?

———

I can never forget or deny that the acts of some of the Southern officials, agents who went into rebellion, were as black, perfidious, forbidding, as any known in history: yet these elements of treachery were exceptional: I regard them as exceptional: after all I am an optimist, I suppose.

Lincoln

No professor—no preacher—can have anything to say about Lincoln. He soars and plays way beyond them all.

The radical element in Lincoln was sadness bordering on melancholy, touched by a philosophy, and that philosophy touched again by a humor, which saved him from the logical wreck of his powers.

———

In long prepared transactions—in arranged, calculated, campaigns—in persevering effort, like Lincoln's, Grant's—towards a great purpose—acknowledging no defeat—there is no luck—no chance. It is like our fine macadamized roads—not the surface alone, but the underpinning—the basis—there is nearly the whole virtue: if that is bad—if the determination of the soil yields—the soil lacks it—all is lost. No one can know as I know how this applies to Lincoln: not enemies at the front alone but in the rear—everywhere—subtle, keen, unscrupulous. I was myself a New Yorker—nestled in the very bone—perhaps not heart, but brain, viscera, of the malcontent—knew it all—from what it came—what was to be expected of it—realized how dark and rapid a weapon it could be. Yet Lincoln, knowing it all, was calm in it all—persevered in his way.

———

Lincoln was not hasty in action—far from it: had almost infinite patience: always waited a long time (an extra long time) before proceeding to extreme measures. He was mighty when aroused. I have seen him both ways—angry as well as calm: more than once seen him when his whole being was shaken up—when his passion was at white heat.

———

Lincoln is like the Bible—you can read anything in him. One man will say, "Here, here, Uncle Abe was so and so—I have the text for it," and another with an opposite notion will say, "See, he was with *us*: I have the text for it."

———

All Lincoln's life was turned to a generous key. When he went to New York, as I have described it, at a time when men's hip-pockets abounded in knives and revolvers—the men only looking for a chance, a pretext, to whip them out, to set the town ablaze, to murder Lincoln, others: at this time, at all later times, Lincoln's policy was, not to offer this opportunity—not to strike this spark. Who can measure the value of such a personality—in its way all-seeing—to America at that time?

———

I should not wonder at any man mistaking Abe Lincoln the first two or three years in Washington: it is very rarely anyhow that men come to know the really great fellows even when they are through, much less when they are in process of making. When men get their calipers out— then what? Nothing very wise, generally. Lincoln was not a specifically great man, as greatness runs in the average mind. He minds me most often of a captain—a great captain—chosen for a tempestuous voyage—everything against him—wind, tide, current, terrible odds—untried seas—balking courses: yet a man equal to all emergencies, never at a loss, quiet, composed, patient—oh how patient!—and coming out at the end, victor—no one in all history more victor! How could the average men know him?—how know Washington—even Grant?—any man of the first class?

———

Lincoln was more Western—his habits so—his dress— speech, but in the things which really establish the hero, the majestic genius, he was Roman, Greek, Biblical—had the towering individuality which peers over all border-lands of race, is one with the great characters of all ages.

———

I remember his cheer, his story-telling—always the good story well told. His ways were beautiful and simple—how well I knew them, watched them! He delighted in simplicity, ruggedness, naturalness, straightforward nativity—in plain habits, clear thinking, doing. And he was the same man in all relationships—for instance, to the boys—the messenger boys—who came often, he would put his hands on their shoulders—say, "My son, is there an answer?" or "Sit down there, my son," something in that way, with a radiant kindliness, humanity—in a natural tone, as if out of a great heart. Though not slangy—not slangy at all—Lincoln was in current without average life—a great, great presence, in our age, our land.

———

No one can really comprehend what Lincoln did unless he understands the great fund of slavery feeling then here at the North as well as that at the South. Indeed, this Northern sympathy was hardest to bear, beset Lincoln with the knottiest problems. This feeling extended not only in a great city like New York, but beyond—for instance, out through the cities of the state (I saw lots of it!)—in Albany, Rochester, Buffalo—in places like Syracuse—so on. And not only among the low and the vile—no, not there—but in Methodistical, Presbyterianistic circles (yes, often with men essentially sound and good). Circles then bad enough, yet with good samples—splendid samples—left, but growing nowadays damnably worse and more vulgar. Lincoln watched, bore with, curbed, all that—never missed the right word, act—led us, in the end, *victors*!

I don't know how there could be anywhere a more conclusive argument in favor of men as they average up than
the life of Lincoln: a life right out of the popular heart—a
hero august and simple as nature—supreme for his own
ends, eligibilities.

———

Lincoln had little or no personal feeling—took every man
at his own measure—accepted—freed—kept the tugging
factions each in place, to do its partial work. That was
Lincoln— full of feeling, none more so—yet not swayed
by feeling. Full of sympathy—using it all—yet the clear-
est-eyed man of them all!

———

Lincoln was pilot of a ship—the storm raged, the stars
were lost—horror, horror, horror! It was not a moment for
abstract right and wrong—for ideal pros and cons—but to
get the ship safe at home—to ride triumphantly into port.

———

Death, murder, pain, assassination—how much they put
into history! Think of Abraham Lincoln, profoundly
constituted throughout as he was—of deep political,
moral, spiritual subtlety, reachings—open to varied influences—everywhere a big man, type, in himself—and
simple—simple as a child in his power—of world-capa-
ciousness—one of the greatest, sweetest souls everyway—

think of him—think how much even Lincoln owes to his taking off, assassination! Immensely much, without a doubt.

Heroes

I think it the necessary thing—I almost pray for it—
that each age should have its hero.

I know that the hero is after all greater than any idealization. Undoubtedly—just as the man is greater than his portrait—the landscape than the picture of it—the fact than anything we can say about the fact. While I accept the records I think we know very little of the actual. I often reflect, how very different every fellow must have been from the fellow we come upon in the myths—with the surroundings, the incidents, the push and pull of the concrete moment, all left out or wrongly set forth. It is hard to extract a man's real self—any man—from such a chaotic mass—from such historical debris.

In our own life here, see how our writers travel and travel and travel for subjects, go into the great west—into forbidden places—or forbidding—lug in hard cases, crimes, criminals, desperadoes—seek out, as I so often say, the delirium tremens of our national life—display that as the essence of it all—us all—passing by in the act all the natural, unheralded heroisms—the nobility of our every-day life—the romance of the streets, courts, palaces, hovels, by-ways, cities, farms, mines. Not but that our actual life has its hard ends to show—its pimps, panders, thieves, bums, whores,—diseases, dirt, smutch, syphilis—enough to answer for all accusations. Though these to me, in the ensemble, the whole, of our life, are small specks: for we need not go into Greece to know the gods—heroes,— Hercules,—all the great figures: here they are, all of them —the equal of the best—waiting at our doors.

———

I envy the man out-of-doors—the boatman in the river, the carter with his team, the farmer at his plough—the active, unliterary employments!—their freedom—the elasticity they develop!

———

I remember the doctors at Washington—and the Generals—especially the Generals—telling me that the greatest heroism, the best marching, the most enduringness, was among men who were under-size—not only under-size, but underweight. The doctors made that report to me in the hospitals: how they liked best, the fellows who would yell, indescribably growl out, moan, fuss, over their wounds—to these there seemed more hope. The quiet men—these the doctors feared for. I remember one man—he was a small man—for whom one of the doctors had serious doubt. The doctor confided to me that the man was a marvel of quiet—was too quiet—had settled into a sort of sweet resignation—though suffering undoubtedly the greatest agony, never made a sign of it—evidently facing the worst undismayed. I can sort of feel how this justifies itself—this growling, howling, yelling—this giving vent to the sensation of the moment: like the opposite of constipation, a sort of clearance, at least for the time being. Yet this is not all—we cannot set out rules: there is one man—there is a second man—a third—so on—all to go by their own impulses, unconstrained.

———

I appeal to no one: I look in all men for the heroic quality I find in Caesar, Carlyle, Emerson: yes indeed—find it, too, it is so surely present. If that is aristocracy then I am an aristocrat.

———

The case of a young fellow suffering from diphtheria: it was a serious case and a serious moment. I urged it on one of the doctors there, a young man, to bathe the patient's throat with a mixture of sweet-oil and chloroform. What did I know about it? It was an uncommon, homely remedy. "I know nothing about it," said the doctor, but added—"No matter for that: I shall try it at once"—which he did and relieved and finally recovered the man. It was to me a rare example of receptiveness. The typical good doctor of the army, than which I know of no better, probably on this globe, united rare sacrifice with deep emotional, sympathetic, qualities—would adapt himself to conditions—was never a medical dogmatist. It is a beautiful thought, the history of which has to me a spice of sacredness—a glimpse of high, however unheralded and unpretentious achievements.

———

Physical heroism was common during the war: indeed, was notable on both sides, in all classes—men and officers, poor and rich, all. This was so rich a quantity that the time came when they needed to be held in, reined—not only the men but the officers, too—officers worse than men, if anything. In all this, brains did not rule—none of it, in fact. As I have often said of the land in America, it is indefinite, infinite—you can call for as much as you want. In true greatness as an accepter of things, Grant, of all men in the War, all leaders, I am inclined to credit most: his composure, adaptedness. For war simply in the concrete—except as it expressed some spiritual fact—my aversion always amounted, amounts to, abhorrence.

———

The great man is not only the man who conceives an idea but the man who can incorporate that idea into practical working human life—of a nation, class, what-not. Bismarck was such a man. Others may have dreamed the unity of Germany—he fulfilled it. We might say as well of

Luther—his great fight against all the devils of earth. No doubt thousands before him had inwardly lived his protest against the Popes: but with him it was death to be silent: he seized the idea—saw that it was concretely realized. He, too, with the greatest, in his own way.

I sometimes think that this is the dark and damned spot of our national character: pettiness, prettiness, quibbling, finery. We have everything—we are big, heroic, grand, smart—oh! as for smartness, *damned* smart! too damned smart: but after our heroism, *this*. And what will come of it? that is the question.

History

My experience with life makes me afraid of the historian:
the historian, if not a liar himself, is largely
at the mercy of liars.

We talk of "facts" in history. What are facts? A good deal
that gets written once is repeated and repeated, until the
future comes to swear by it as a gospel.

———

We get into such grooves—that's the trouble—passing
traditions and exaggerations down from one generation
to another unquestioned. After awhile we begin to think
even the lies must be true.

———

[Matthew] Brady had galleries in Washington: his head-
quarters were in New York. We had many a talk together:
the point was, how much better it would often be, rather
than having a lot of contradictory records by witnesses or
historians—say of Caesar, Socrates, Epictetus, others—if
we could have three or four or half a dozen portraits—
very accurate—of the men: that would be history—

the best history—a history from which there could be no appeal.

———

I have something of Shelley's distaste for history—so much of it is cruel, so much of it is lie. I am waiting for the historians who will tell the truth about the people—about the nobility of the people: the essential soundness of the common man. There are always—there have been always—a thousand good deeds that we say nothing about for every bad deed that we fuss over. Think of the things in everyday life—we see them everywhere—that never are exploited in print. Nobody hunts them up—nobody puts them into a story. But let one base thing happen and all the reporters of all the papers are on the spot in a minute. That don't seem to give goodness a fair deal—though I don't know: maybe goodness don't need a fair deal—maybe goodness gets along on its own account without the historian.

———

All the "great phases" in history are no doubt fictions.

———

People little know how less than a thousandth part—a thousandth thousandth part—of things written, prepared, studied, gets into print. All that goes to the making of what is published is unknown—ever must be unknown. And it is a vast sea of itself. Oh the tragedy and pathos of it!

———

I find I can write, master, cope with affairs fifty years old better than with those occurring now: I get more completely the sense of proportion.

———

Could a truthful history of anything, of any individual, be told? A truthful history of an individual means to bring out folly, mistake, error, crime, devilishness, poison. Who can do that? Who could even write a history of our own Rebellion—a truthful history, even if he dared?

———

The thing to have is the truth, not to be satisfied even with the *spirit* of truth, but to demand the fact itself—the divine, unaided, uncircumlocuted, unmanipulated fact, however bare, however it forbids—only in an adherence to this is the safety of history.

Biography

It is hard to extract a man's real self—any man—from such a chaotic mass—from such historical debris.

I meet new Walt Whitmans every day. There are a dozen of me afloat. I don't know which Walt Whitman I am. Now, there's Abraham Lincoln: people get to know his traits, his habits of life, some of his characteristics set off in the most positive relief: soon all sorts of stories are fathered on him—some of them true, some of them apocryphal—volumes of stories (stories decent and indecent) fathered on him: legitimate stories, illegitimate: and so Lincoln comes to us more or less falsified.

———

After all, nothing makes up a good deal of a man's life: these trifles are registers, explanations, confirming, justifying.

———

I have hated so much of the biography in literature because it is so untrue: look at our national figures how they are spoiled by liars: by the people who think they can improve on God Almighty's work—who put an extra touch on here, there, here again, there again, until the real man is no longer recognizable.

———

I know how, after a man disappears, the mists begin to gather, then fallacy of one degree or another, then utter myth, irresistibly mystifying everything. It is a lamentable twist in history.

Politics and Politicians

*The best politics that could happen for our republic
would be the abolition of politics.*

In politics—just as it is in religion—some people get an
idea of the necessity of believing certain things, not so
much from weight of evidence, out or in,—but from mere
mental and emotional set-ness: they intend believing—
and that all there is about it!

———

Washington is corrupt—has its own peculiar mixture of
evil with its own peculiar mixture of good—but the evil
is mostly with the upper crust—the people who have reputations—who are better than other people.

———

Unhappy the country without a party of the opposition—though there are oppositions and oppositions. Even
Washington is examined—needs to be examined. I do not
mean by a party of the opposition such parties as we have
today—but a party!

———

I don't know what the unspeakable rush for money means—will lead to—on this continent. Unmentionable degradation—rottenness—the foulest, perhaps, taking it politically, ever known, ever written of in history. Wealth unbounded, greed as unbounded, one man feasting on the ruins of another! Look at politics—stinking, dripping, with the last filth, experiences.

———

I think the world has never paid enough deference to that principle of Quakers, which, in their meetings, prevents a mere majority from deciding policies, actions. One vote or several not being sufficient to make a rule operative. Always suggesting to me a silent sweet deference to minorities, to the spirit; not doing all out of awe of numbers. I am sure it is a rebuking contrast to all that is accepted in the methods of legislation.

———

Start with Washington: come down to our own day—to Cleveland: the selection of men from the first to last registered a certain average of success. We are too apt to pause with particulars: the Presidency has a significance, a meaning, broader, higher, than could be imparted to it by any individual however spacious, satisfying. There is no great importance attaching to Presidents regarding them simply as individuals put into the chair after a partisan fight: the Presidency stands for a profounder fact: consider that: detached from that it is an incumbrance indeed, not a lift, to the spirit. We need to enclose the principle of the Presidency in this conception: here is the summing up, the essence, the eventuation, of the will of sixty millions of people of all races, colors, origins, inextricably intermixed: for true or false the sovereign statement of the popular hope.

———

In our own town—uptown—all that half of the place— are a lot of people—cultured, cute, moneyed, colleged, prosperous, arrayed in purple and fine linen, satisfied with their books—who, I venture to say, pay their taxes, knowing they are looted—but half of whom couldn't tell you today who is mayor of the city. Yet America, robbed, gnawed at the vitals, lived upon by a mass of corrupting political fraud—is wealthiest of the list—exceeds all in her power to outlast her evils.

Aaron Burr

Do you know much about Aaron Burr? There's a man, now, who is only damned and damned again in history and yet who had his parts. I have always designed writing something about him to show I did not stand in the jam of his vilifiers. I had a piece on him which should have gone into this book. You don't know (I guess I never told you) that when I was a lad, working in a lawyer's office, it fell to me to go over the river now and then with messages for Burr. Burr was very gentle—persuasive. He had a way of giving me a bit of fruit on these visits—an apple or a pear. I can see him clearly, still—his stateliness, gray hair, courtesy, consideration.

Zachary Taylor

General Taylor—afterwards the President. In New Orleans—forty years ago—about the close of the Mexican War—I came to know him there. A plain man—without the first sign of airishness—yet a man with his entourage of slaves—a man used to being served—military—a disciplinarian, yet a jolly man—fond of a good story—living well—realizing life. As plain as Grant, yet more frank and outspoken.

Horace Greeley

Greeley was pale—had no color in his eye, no color in his cheek, no color in his hair. Greeley's great consuming trait—seizing and subordinating all other traits—was his smartness—his ability to occupy the smart side of things, every time. It is the New England gift.

Charles Sumner

I knew Sumner. I had spent a good deal of time in the South, off and on. Sumner seemed to know about it—once suggested that I should give him my impressions of Southern life and character. I went to Sumner but he would not stand for me—not a damned bit of it. My view of the South was a little bit favorable—this seemed to irritate him: he would not have it so: stormed, stormed, would not yield a point. I have no doubt there is just as much chivalry, consideration, of its own kind, north here as south—in expressing some approbation of the southern social spirit I did not intend to accuse Yankeedom. But Sumner would not have the applause on any terms—cast it out of court.

———

Sumner was a big man—a noble-looking one, too: large—imposing. All Sumner's bases were right, sound, secure, but there was elegance, artificiality about him in unmistakable quantity—parts for which you and I, for instance, would criticize him, would differ. I should say, that things original—any real hospitality for inherencies—no, they were not for him, he shrank from them. Yet that is to state it strongly, too, for there was that to be said, then more: then something of the native pluck, strength, faith of the man. But Sumner had that damnable Yankee accessory—the shudder, for a word misspelled, misused, a false intonation. Even Emerson had it.

Andrew Johnson

Every man, whatever may have been his antecedents, whatever he had been before—what his origins, associations—the instant he takes the Presidential chair does his damnedest best, his damnedest best, to justify those who elevated him to the office. I believe this even of Andy Johnson—in many respects the least likeable of the lot: I was near him: my position in the Attorney General's Office placed me in almost daily contact with those who were close to him: even Johnson went according to his light, though his light flickered enough and was often near to going out, to be sure.

Ulysses S. Grant

I was still in Washington while Grant was President. I saw a good deal of him about the city. He went quite freely everywhere alone. I remember one spot in particular where I often crossed him—a little cottage on the outskirts of Washington: he was frequently there—going there often. I learned that an old couple of whom he was very fond lived there. He had met them in Virginia—they received him in a plain democratic way: I would see him leaning on their window sills outside: all would be talking together: they seeming to treat him without deference for place—with dignity, courtesy, appreciation.

———

Grant's great feature was his entire reserve—his reserve behind reserve: his horse sense, I may say: he never set himself apart in an atmosphere of greatness: he always remained the same plain man—the unwavering democrat.

Benjamin Harrison

Let me predict this—that as long as Harrison remains in office, the aura of the Presidency will give him prominence—be his savior—but after that—oh! what will be his oblivion!—utter!

Radicals

Although my philosophy includes conservatives,
everything else being equal I prefer the radicals
as men and companions.

I think the fellows who rouse us and taunt us—perhaps
even torment us—are the most valuable in some respects.

I am a radical of radicals   but I don't belong to any school.

I am as radical now as ever—just as radical—but I am
not asleep to the fact that among radicals as among the
others there are hoggishnesses, narrownesses, inhuman-
ities, which at times almost scare me for the future—for
the future belongs to the radical and I want to see him do
good things with it.

The most of things history has to say about [Thomas]
Paine are damnably hideous. The polite circles of that
period and later on were determined to queer the reputation of contemporary radicals—not Paine alone, but

others also—Fanny Wright, [Joseph] Priestly, for instance. The young radicals of that time have never had justice done them: they rallied—such of them as were in New York—about Paine and were far in advance of their time. Paine himself did signal, lasting work—work to which our people have been disgracefully oblivious.

———

[William Lloyd] Garrison always spoke like a man who had a story to tell and was determined to tell it: he never seemed to have any doubts about the splendor and efficacy of his doctrine. He was of the noblest race of revolutionaries—a man who could accept without desiring martyrdom: he always seemed to me to belong where he was—never seemed gratuitous: the splendid band of his companions never found their confidence in him misplaced. Like all men of the real sort he was modest, simple—never had to look beyond his natural self and employ the artificial weapons of rebellion. I rank Garrison way up: I don't know how high, but very high.

———

Great figures, every way, contending for reforms—the anti-slavery men greatest, more momentous—temperance, too—and the woman rightsers. Real giant fights. Those temperance fellows who thought rum was accountable for all the woes of man—who even dignified this by thinking it a *principle*. . . . But on the whole the anti-slavery

men took off the honors. They were so deadly in earnest—
so many of them such grand speakers!

———

I, for my part, could never see in [John] Brown himself,
merely of himself, the evidence of great human quality:
yet Emerson said when they killed Brown: "Now you have
made the gallows as holy as the cross." That was sublime,
ultimate, everlasting: yet they will not permit us to say
Emerson was extreme.

———

In those days I fell in mostly with abolitionists—rabid
abolitionists noble, big fellows, many of them, but all
consumed by the notion, which I never would admit, that
slavery—slavery alone—was evil, and the universe con-
tained no other.

———

Look at Wendell Phillips—great and grand as he was:
with him light and darkness were all for the one ill and
that alone—all: he was one-eyed, saw nothing, absolutely
nothing, but that single blot of slavery. And if Phillips of
old, others today.

———

The abolitionists have always exaggerated the importance
of that movement: it was not by any means the beginning

or end of things. It was a pimple, a boil—yes, a carbuncle—that's it—out of the nation's bad blood: out of a corpus spoiled, maltreated, bruised, poisoned. The Southerners, by acts of folly—acts like that of beating down Sumner—added to the fuel.

———

I often question myself if we—if I myself, for one—make enough allowance for the swelling and swelling and swelling and rising tide of radicalism of our time—radicalism everywhere, overflowing churches, states, institutions everywhere. Whether after all an absolute majority of the millions of people now in this America—our America—is not radical, more or less, knowing or unknowing?

———

We are not going to be reformed in this way, by parcels—not by Henry Georgian Socialism, Anarchism, Schools—any one agency.

Internationalism

*Can any sound man believe in a patriotism
that means America alone?*

America means above all toleration, catholicity, welcome,
freedom—a concern for Europe, for Asia, for Africa,
along with its concern for America. It is something quite
peculiar, hardly to be stated—evades you as the air—yet
is a fact everywhere preciously present.

———

Restrict nothing—keep everything open: to Italy, to
China, to anybody. I love America, I believe in America, because her belly can hold and digest all—anarchist,
socialist, peacemakers, fighters, disturbers or degenerates
of whatever sort—hold and digest all. If I felt that America could not do this I would be indifferent as between
our institutions and any others. America is not all in all—
the sum total: she is only to contribute her contribution
to the big scheme. What shall that contribution be? I say,
let it be something worth while—something exceptional,
ennobling.

———

While I seem to love America, and wish to see America prosperous, I do not seem able to bring myself to love America, to desire American prosperity, at the expense of some other nation or even of all other nations.

———

The theory of the progress and expansion of the cause of the common bulk of the people is the same in all countries,—not only in the British islands, but on the continent of Europe and allwheres,—that we are all embarked together like fellows in a ship, bound for good or for bad. What wrecks one wrecks all. What reaches the port for one reaches the port for all. And it is my feeling, and I hope I have in *Leaves of Grass* expressed it, that the bulk of the common people, the torso of the people, the great body of the people all over the civilized world,—and any other, too, for that matter,—are sailing, sailing together in the same ship.

———

America now should stand for the world—should bear witness not only to her own success, but human solidarity, universal union, the largest possible circle of comradeship.

———

The idea of a universal language is grand, noble—is in line with all the broad, deep, tendencies of the time—is one with our political progress—governments, free trade,

solidarity—the democratic drifts, glories, of our time—
the over-flowing, ever-flowing, humanities!

———

Language is a thing which takes its own path of growth—
may some day merge all tongues into one tongue but will
not do so by an edict of scholars or a pronunciamento from
the universities. A universal language has a lot to provide
for—must provide for the Asiatic and the African as well
as for us—must not cast out any nation, any people, however remote. I do not say a universal language may not
grow but I am sure it cannot be deliberately made piecemeal by scholastic machinery.

———

It is very easy to get up a hurrah—call it freedom, patriotism: but none of that is patriotism in any sense I accept.

———

Solidarity, intercalation: not Philadelphia alone, Camden
alone, even New York alone, but all together, all nations:
the globe: intercalation, fusion, no one left out.

———

Solidarity, unifying—unification! This is in fact my argument for free trade—not that it will produce so much
and so much in dollars—though that too is to be said,
and I feel that free trade could be justified even on that

ground—but that it will break down partitions, dividing lines—lines of demarkation—bring the race together—interests not worldly alone, but on the human side—the high deep embracing spiritualities.

Science

Oh! The great Darwin! None greater in our time!
Big—big—big! I for one am grateful to have lived
as one of his contemporaries.

I should be inclined to say the supreme value, the highest service, science is rendering to thought, today, in our world, is in clearing the way, pioneering, opening roads: untilling, in fact, some things instead of tilling them: sweeping away, destroying, burning, the underbrush.

——————

I like the scientific spirit—the holding off, the being sure but not too sure, the willingness to surrender ideas when the evidence is against them: this is ultimately fine—it always keeps the way beyond open—always gives life, thought, affection, the whole man, a chance to try over again after a mistake—after a wrong guess.

——————

The crowning characteristic, the final glory, of our age is in this—that it is an age of inquiry: inquiry that enters everything—everything sacred or profane: with no spot anywhere but someone wants to explore it. I know every age is in some measure an age of inquiry, but I don't think there ever was an age that so daringly, so persistently, everywhere, insisted upon its right to investigate.

———

I have great faith in science—real science: the science that is the science of the soul as well as the science of the body (you know many men of half sciences seem to forget the soul).

———

It always amazes me when a man of science drifts off into materialism: I look to every man of science to maintain the assertion of omnipresent unmitigated never terminable life: when he does anything else I suspect him of being false to his standards of truth. This may sound like inexcusable dogmatism, though I offer it in any but a dogmatic spirit.

———

I stand in awe before the men of science: they hold the key to the situation: they are the true discoverers: they are—they, with their utter abandon, honesty.

———

Darwin is to me science incarnate; its spirit is Darwin.

———

Doctors after all seem of all professional men to be the most in accord with the givings-out of science: more in line with the new truths, new spirit: less given to professional dead-headery, foppery: more interested in fundamentals. In all the other professions men lag behind. The doctor is certainly better than the lawyer—oh! far better: the lawyer is buried deep in red-taperies, dead phraseologies, antique precedents: not in what is right now but in what has been done before: a species of stagnation overcomes him. The doctors are way ahead—far beyond all that.

After culture has said its last say we find that the best things yet remain to be said: that the heart is still listening to have heart things said to it—the brain still listening to have brain things said to it—the faith, the spirit, the soul of man waiting to have such things of faith, spirit, the soul, said to it. Books won't say what we must have said: try all that books may they can't say it. The utmost pride goes with the utmost resignation: science says to us—be ready to say yes whatever happens, whatever don't happen: yes, yes, yes. That's where science becomes religion—where the new spirit utters the highest truth—makes the last demonstration of faith: looks the universe full in the face—its bad in the face, its good—and says yes to it.

Religion

After you have got rid of all your dogmas then you can read the Bible—realize its immensity—not till then.

I claim everything for religion: after the claims of my religion are satisfied nothing is left for anything else: yet I have been called irreligious—an infidel (God help me!): as if I could have written a word of the *Leaves* without its religious root-ground. I am not traditionally religious—I know it: but even traditionally I am not anti: I take all the old forms and faiths and remake them in conformity with the modern spirit, not rejecting a single item of the earlier programs.

I think the first five centuries of Christianity very precious and necessary to the history of humanity. It came as a protest against a too great leaning in one direction—a too great tendency—exclusive tendency—towards militarism: among the Greeks to mere beauty. In an era which could acknowledge nothing but the military virtues—which, high as they are, are not by any means the highest—it came, filled great niches, wide gaps—furnished a purifying, freshening of the race. I should say of it as

I might of our Rebellion here in America: our Rebellion confirmed, justified, explicated America: Christianity confirmed, justified, explicated humanity.

———◆———

The true Jesus? who, what, was the true Jesus: I can't tell: can you? The story, what we know of it, is so faded, so pale, as well as so manufactured (almost theatrical), that we can form no definite idea, no plausible estimate, of what Jesus can have been like.

———◆———

I often get mad at the ministers—they are almost the only people I do get mad at—yet they, too, have their reasons for being. If a man will once consent to be a minister he must expect ruin.

———◆———

I have not been without friends even among the Catholics. I have had friends in the priesthood—half a dozen of them. So far concerns the Catholic church, however, I have had in the main to look at it from the outside—I have seen a little of its pageantry and read with deep interest of the royal, gorgeous, superb displays in the cathedrals, especially those down in Rome—in St. Peter's. It is grand, grand—O how grand! Yet it has one defect: it lacks simplicity—it has deferred too much to certain sensational elements in its history and environment.

———

I could tell you of a wonderful experience—of a related but dissimilar experience—of an incident in which all the integers were simple—were more directly related to life. It was in Washington, during the war, in one of the wards of a hospital—a poor room, with cheaper furniture than this you see in my parlor, which is poor enough: a three legged stool for an altarpiece—no light but the light of a candle: then a priest came and administered the sacrament to a poor soldier. The room was spare, blank—no furnishings: the hearers in the other beds seemed altogether incredulous or else altogether convinced: there was a suspicion of quackery, humbuggery, in the whole performance: no one among the observers except myself perhaps was respectful. I stood aside and watched, aroused in places to sympathy, though mainly impressed by the spectacular features of the event—by its human emotional features. All was done solemnly, without noise—done in a way to appeal to your sense of right weight and measure—proportion, proportion. It is necessary for you to know with what sort of emphasis such an incident affected me if you want to get a just perception of my esthetics. No magnificent cathedral could quite so well have rounded up my simple picture. I remember another scene—a regiment, once made up of a thousand or twelve hundred men, returned from the war—from the battles, sieges, skirmishings, halts, marches, goings on—coming into Washington, perhaps on an errand only, for provisioning—God knows what:

only there on duty for a day or more: now reduced from its proud twelve hundred to its humble one or two hundred men, trailing in, as it may be said, what remained of them, with their colors in rags and their faces emaciated, worn, but with their hearts true. Don't that beat a cathedral picture? I think it does—God! it does, it does! It makes your heart bleed. Then you worship—get down on your real knees.

The idea of the ministers seems to be, that without the theory of heaven and hell—particularly of hell—society would not be safe—things would not go on—we would collapse!

Damn the preachers! what do they know or care to know? The churches have constructed a god of moral goodness—wholly, solely, moral goodness—and that is its weakness. For if there is one thing that is *not* true, that is the thing: not but that moral goodness has its part. See what we get out of science, democracy, the modern—on this point! According to such a standard of moral goodness—the standard of the churches—probably nine-tenths of the universe is depraved—probably nine-tenths denied a right in the scheme of things—which is ridiculous, outright: might have satisfied an older intelligence, but will not ours. Our time, land, age, the future—demands readjustment—demands the fuller recognition of democracy—the *ensemble*: these have hardly been recognized at all in the old theology. What can science have to do with such a spectre as the present church? All their methods are opposed—must be opposed—utterly opposed: for one means restriction, the other freedom: the church—ill-adjustment, science—harmony.

———

Sunday—Sunday: we make it the dullest day in the week when it might be made the cheeriest. Will the people ever come to base-ball, plays, concerts, yacht races, on Sundays? That would seem like clear weather after a rain. Why do you suppose people are so narrow-minded in their interpretation of the Sunday? If we read about Luther we find that he was not gloomy, not sad-devout, not sickly-religious: but a man full of blood who didn't hesitate to outrage ascetic customs or play games if he felt like it on Sunday. The Catholic regards Sunday with a more nearly sane eye. It does seem as though the Puritan was responsible for our Sunday: the Puritan had his virtues but I for one owe him a grudge or two which I don't hesitate to talk about loud enough to be heard.

———

The damnable psalming, praying, deaconizing of our day is made too much the liberal cover for all sorts of sins, iniquities.

I anticipate the day when some wise man will start out to argue that two and two are not four but five or something else: history proving that two and two couldn't be four: and probability, too: yes, more than that, the wise man will prove it out of his own consciousness—prove it for somebody—for a few: they will believe in him—a body of disciples will believe: then, presto! you have a new religion!

God? Well, there are other divinities: they are not of the hell and damnation sort: they are not of the legs and arms sort—the personal sort: they yet remain, more firmly on their thrones, in the race, than ever: they continue their supremacy.

God Almighty is very high-falutin! All his ways, globes, habits—high-falutin! I suppose in all our millions of population—our 80 millions—teeming, spreading—there are not a dozen men—not a dozen, even—who realize— really realize,—realize in the sense of absolutely picturing, nearing, participating in it—vibrating, pulsing—that this earth we inhabit is whirling about in space at the rate of thousands of miles a minute—going on in a hell of a way: that his earth is but one of a cluster of earths—these clusters of clusters of clusters again—and all again, again, again, circulating, whirling about a central system, fact, principle—movement everywhere incessant immense, over-whelming. Now—I doubt if there are a dozen men who really sketch that to themselves—perceive, embrace, what it means—comprehend in the midst of what a high-falu-tin extravagant creation we live, exist. And yet things go on and on—keeping up their high-falutin course!

———

A religion? Well—every man has a religion: has some-thing in heaven or earth which he will give up everything else for—something which absorbs him, possesses itself of him, makes him over into its image: something: it may be something regarded by others as being very paltry, inade-quate, useless: yet it is his dream, it is his lodestar, it is his master.

Mystery, Faith, and the Universe

I never believe in the impossible. I accept the saying
of some witty Frenchman—that the impossible
is the likeliest thing to happen.

Mystery is not the denial of reason but its honest confirmation: reason, indeed, leads inevitably to mystery—but, as you know, mystery is not superstition: mystery and reality are the two halves of the same sphere.

———

When it comes to explaining absolute beginnings, ends, I doubt if evolution clears up the mystery any better than the philosophies that have preceded it. I have felt from the first that my own work must assume the essential truths of evolution, or something like them.

———

I think there is a damnable disposition sometimes to deny, to affront, the substance, the spirit, the life, the joy, of things.

———

I have very little room for the man who disdains the universe. One of my first questions is always that—not always spoken—not methodically *thought*, even—but in a way taking its measure: do you, or you, *accept* the universe and all that is in it? It is an important question.

———

Whether it is constitutional or what-not with me, I stand for the sunny point of view—stand for the joyful conclusions. This is not because I merely guess: it's because my faith seems to belong to the nature of things—is imposed, cannot be escaped: can better account for life and what goes with life than the opposite theory.

———

I am not prepared to admit fraud in the scheme of the universe—yet without immortality all would be sham and sport of the most tragic nature. I remember, also, what Epictetus said: What is good enough for the universe is good enough for me!—immortality for the universe, immortality is good enough for me! These are not reasons—not reasons: they are impressions, visions. What the world calls logic is beyond me: I only go about my business taking on impressions—reporting impressions—though sometimes I imagine that what we see is superior to what we reason about—what establishes itself in the age, in the heart, is finally the only logic—can boast of the only real verification.

———

I get very impatient some days—am a little resentful: sore, sore: wonder if it's all fair and square—whether the scheme after all is not doubtful: then I go back: find my way back to my central thought again—my spinal conviction: I resent my resentment—am ashamed of my questions. Oh! I feel how empty everything would seem if I was not full of this faith—if this faith did not overthrow me: how useless all things would be if they led on to nothing but what we see—to nothing but what we appear to wind up in here.

———

The greatest lesson of all—the supreme—is that this great earth—swinging in its orbit—freighted with life, mystery, beauty—going round, round, round points everywhere to an indescribable good—goes on, on—we do not know to what, but we feel to just ends. Oh! an indefinably august power enclosing, explaining, all.

———

In my periods of trouble—when I am sleepless—lie awake thinking, thinking, of things I ought not to think about at all—am frustrated—worried. Then I recover by centering all attention on the starry system—the orbs, globes—the vast spaces—the perpetual, perpetual, perpetual flux and flow—method, inevitability, dependability of the cosmos.

It excites wonder, reverence, composure—I am always rendered back to myself.

———

As I grow older I am more firmly than ever fixed in my belief that all things tend to good, that no bad is forever bad, that the universe has its own ends to subserve and will subserve them well.

Immortality

There are senses in which we do not know—
I know and I don't know.

I believe in immortality, and by that I mean *identity*. I know I have arrived at this result more by what may be called feeling than formal reason—but I believe it: yes, I know it. I am easily put to flight, I assure you, when attacked, but I return to the faith, inevitably—believe it, and stick to it, to the end. Emerson somewhere speaks of encountering irresistible logic and yet standing fast to his conviction. There is judgment back of judgment—defeat only seems like defeat: there is a fierce fight: the smoke is gone—your enemies are nowhere to be seen—you are placidly victorious after all—the finish of the day is yours. Logic does very little for me: my enemies say it, meaning one thing—I say it, meaning another thing.

———

Schiller's idea is the only one for modern science—that if it is right, immortality will come; if not right, not.

My Philosophy

I am more likely to have feelings than theories about things:
I was never a man to drive doctrines to death—to take up
with fads, special providences, whims of diet or manners.

The last thing the world needs is a cut and dried philosophy, and that last man to announce a cut and dried philosophy would be Walt Whitman. Why, boy, there's just the secret of it—which you have always so well grasped: including all philosophies, as I do, how could I nail myself to any one, or single specimen—except it be this, only— that my philosophy is to include all other philosophies.

———

My philosophy sees a place and a time for everybody— even Judas Iscariot—yes, for all: all of us are parties to the same bargain: the worst, the best, the middling—all parties to the same bargain.

———

That is my contention: not to make wholesale comparisons, draw rigid lines, put everybody into a scale, try every man by a tape measure: I take it to be one of the main things if not the main thing, implied by my philosophy, if I may so dignify it, that there is no one man anywhere—that there are countless men on all sides, in all countries, who contribute to the great result—most of them in fact without a name, unknown, eclipsed by the formidable reputations of mostly lesser people. It's queer, sad, disconcerting—how that goes: it can't be helped: but we should contribute nothing ourselves to such a falsifying human habit.

———

When it comes to launching out into mathematics—tying philosophy to the multiplication table—I am lost—lost utterly. Let them all whack away—I am satisfied: if they can explain, let them explain: if they can explain they can do more than I can do. I am not Anarchist, not Methodist, not anything you can name. Yet I see why all the ists and isms and haters and dogmatists exist—can see why they must exist and why I must include all.

———

We must not give too much importance to personalism—it is easy to overcharge it—man moves as man, in all the great achievements—man in the great mass: yet I, too, think of Lincoln much in that same way: as you say, his poise, his simple, loftiest ability to make an emergency sacred, meet every occasion—never shrinking, never failing, never hurrying—these are things to be remembered and things "providential" if "providence" ever has a meaning in human affairs.

———

People think an event consists of itself alone—but what event is there but involves a thousand elements scarcely dreamed of?

———

We must not look back over our shoulders at the world: we should meet each day as it comes with the same assumption: we can make each new day the best of days if we get the habit.

———

Epicurus, all the big fellows, the sages, then, now, always keep themselves free for new impressions—new lights. Look at Emerson saying: "This is so and so—seems so and so to me to-day: what will happen to-morrow I cannot tell." There was Darwin, too—I always put the two together: Emerson, Darwin: Darwin was sweetly, grandly non-opinionative.

———

We must be resigned, but not too much so: we must be calm, but not too calm: we must not give in—yet we must give in some: that is, we must grade our rebellion and our conformity—both.

———

I remember that a long time ago, down at Timber Creek —I would go along the stream, looking, singing, reciting, reading, ruminating—and one fellow there—a splendid sapling—I would take in my hands—pull back—so-so: let it fly, as it did with a will, into position again—its uprightness. One day I stopped in the exercise, the thought striking me: this is great amusement to me: I wonder if not as great to the sapling? It was a fruitful pause: I never forgot it: nor *answered* it. I suppose—this is a new strophe— Montaigne in other dress.

———

I do not teach a definite philosophy—I have no cocked and primed system—but I outline, suggest, hint—tell what I see—then each may make up the rest for himself. He who goes to my book expecting a cocked and primed philosophy, will depart utterly disappointed—and deserve to! I find anyhow that a great many of my readers credit my writings with things that do not attach to the writings themselves but to the persons who read them—things they supply, bring with them.

———

Epictetus says: "Do not let yourself be wrapt by phantasms"—and we must not: that is very profound: it often comes back to me.

———

Epictetus is the one of all my old cronies who has lasted to this day without cutting a diminished figure in my perspective. He belongs with the best—the best of great teachers—is a universe in himself. He sets me free in a flood of light—of life, of vista.

———

My contention is for the whole man—the whole corpus— not one member—not a leg, an arm, a belly alone, but the entire corpus, nothing left out of the account. I know it will be argued that the present is the time of specialization, but that don't answer it.

Spirituality

*I believe in the eligibility of the human soul
for all perfect things.*

It is not in forms, institutions, railroads, telegraphs, factories, stores—all our parades—no, no: these are but fleeting ephemera—these alone are nothing, absolutely nothing; only the absorbent spirit enveloping, penetrating, going beneath, above, all—only *this* is something. And a ferment on the surface—how little it may mean! And *observations*—how short the road they lead us!

———◆———

Take the average of men—take measure of the great qualities in what is called the mass of our population—and you find in fact an elevation never achieved before. And this despite all the acknowledged bad, the evils, the poisonous tendencies. And this, too, as applying not only to worldly situations, conditions, so-called, but what we call gifts, benefits, of mind, the spiritual endowment.

———◆———

[Giuseppe] Mazzini puts his own case in a noble way: he has enthusiasm: without that, what is a man? I don't think there can be any great character, really great character, without centrality—some prevailing idea, some purpose at heart: more and more that conviction possesses me, absorbs me.

———

The Quaker nativity seems to tell, somehow—the absence of too great artificiality—a certain sort of almost impossibility to make-believe. I think the Quaker—the typical Quaker—is a certain sort of materialist—they like the world, and all that: but a certain spirituality remains—a purity, aspiration. After all that is said and done—a Quaker can hardly be without *some* of this—whatever the form of belief: and his materiality is itself his own—like bathing, keeping clean and all that.

———

[*Leaves of Grass*] stands first of all for that something back of phenomena, in phenomena, which gives it all its significance, yet cannot be described—which eludes definition, yet is the most real thing of all.

Success

No life is a failure.

It is a new experience to be successful: I always seem to know what to do with failure but success is a puzzle to me.

————

If men only knew that they were to become great—as they never do—how well they might prepare for it! Start in youth, fill the table drawers with poems, stories, whatever: then, when fame is on, and the editors will take most of anything a man writes, bring 'em out!

————

I have done the work: I have thrown my life into the work: in those early years: teaching, loafing, working on the newspapers: traveling: then in Washington—clerking, nursing the soldiers: putting my life into the scale—my single simple life: putting it up for what it was worth: into the book: pouring it into the book: honestly, without stint, giving the book all, all, all.

————

My worst struggle was not with ideas, anything of that sort, but against the literariness of the age—for I, too, like all others, was born in the vesture of this false notion of literature, and no one so born can entirely—I say entirely—escape the taint. Though, as for me, looking back on the battleground, I pride myself I have escaped the pollution as much as any.

Aging

We pass through days—like eras—of the commonplace.
But the commonplace is grand, too!

I like the boys who are glad they are boys—the men who remain boys. Why should any man ever give up being a boy?

———

I don't say a man's old age is as important as his youth or less important than his youth: or his work—that it's as strong: that does not come in: I only say that in the larger view, in the scheme originally laid down for the *Leaves,* the last old age even if an old age of the dotard is as essential (if I live to old age) as the record of my first youth.

———

When did I not look old? At twenty-five or twenty-six they used already to remark it.

———

There's no rule for old age—a man comes to his nineties if he comes, not otherwise!

———

What a wonder it is—living still—living still—coming here out of the stages of babyhood. What more helpless creature is on this whole orb than the newborn baby—yet I am here, held on and on—from that stage and stage, stage, stage since. Is it not a wonder—a wonder?

———

One's life is not always the thing it is supposed to be—has its periods and periods—dark, light, dark again—spots, errors, damned foolishnesses. Looking back over my own time—looking into the period starting with '61–'62—I have nothing to regret, nothing to wish reversed. But then, it might be asked—why is it, just when a man gets his height, his purpose, begins to live, comes the thwarting signs, the hedging-ins, the breakups, the ending? Why is it?

———

For a while I may fight off the end—for a little space I may hold the city: but the enemy is strong and valiant—is sure of victory—my only hope, to keep comfortable as I can and do what I may as long as I may, going down at last without disgrace.

———

Now, in these late days, as I look back upon the past, I can see that, in a sense, my misfortunes have been my fortunes—that it must have been altogether right for me to have travelled a rough, hard road—so to be tested, at last secured!

—————

My work is done. Nothing remains now but to ring the curtain down.

Sources

All passages are taken from Horace Traubel, *With Walt Whitman in Camden*, published in nine volumes over a ninety-year span:

Vol. 1 (March 28 to July 14, 1888): Boston: Small, Maynard, 1906.

Vol. 2 (July 16 to October 31, 1888): New York: D. Appelton, 1908.

Vol. 3 (November 1, 1888, to January 20, 1889): New York: Mitchell Kennerley, 1914.

Vol. 4 (January 21 to April 7, 1889), ed. Sculley Bradley: Philadelphia: University of Pennsylvania Press, 1953.

Vol. 5 (April 8 to September 14, 1889), ed. Gertrude Traubel: Carbondale: Southern Illinois University Press, 1964.

Vol. 6 (September 15, 1889, to July 6, 1890), ed. Gertrude Traubel and William White: Carbondale: Southern Illinois University Press, 1982.

Vol. 7 (July 7, 1890, to February 10, 1891), ed. Jeanne Chapman and Robert MacIsaac: Carbondale: Southern Illinois University Press, 1992.

Vol. 8 (February 11 to September 30, 1891), ed. Jeanne

Chapman and Robert MacIsaac: Oregon House, CA: William Bentley, 1996.

Vol. 9 (October 1, 1891, to April 3, 1892), ed. Jeanne Chapman and Robert MacIsaac: Oregon House, CA: William Bentley, 1996.

*The text in this book is set in 10 point Granjon, a font
created for Linotype in the late 1920s by British type designer
George W. Jones (1860–1942), who used as his models two
French typefaces from the late sixteenth century: a roman
cut designed by Claude Garamond and an italic by
Robert Granjon—thus the name. The paper is an acid-free
Forest Stewardship Council–certified stock that exceeds
the requirements for permanence of the American National
Standards Institute. The binding material is Arrestox, a cotton-based
cloth with an aqueous acrylic coating manufactured by
Holliston, Church Hill, Tennessee. Text design and composition
by Gopa & Ted2, Inc., Albuquerque, New Mexico.
Printing and binding by McNaughton & Gunn, Saline,
Michigan, with jackets furnished by Phoenix Color,
Hagerstown, Maryland.*